LET'S PARTY!

Gluten-Free
Entertaining
for Everyone

LET'S PARTY!

Gluten-Free Entertaining for Everyone

Monika Sudakov

*Hither
Page
Press*

*Princeton,
Illinois*

Editor: Paula Morrow
Book Designer: Ron McCutchan
Printed in the United States of America

Library of Congress Control Number: 2010916619

ISBN-13: 978-09798332-6-7

I would like to dedicate this book to
two different groups of people.
First of all, to all of our wonderful guests who have passed
through our doors over the course of the last 6 years who had
gluten intolerances. You challenged me and reminded me why
this endeavor is important and necessary in this day and age.

Secondly and most importantly, I would like to
dedicate this book to my mother-in-law, Roz.
Her diagnosis may have changed her life but it also changed
mine. I had a very personal reason to learn about celiac disease
and to create recipes that I knew she could enjoy. More than
anything I wanted for her to feel like she was included when
we entertained. I wanted her to know she was important and
special and didn't want her to feel left out. I knew that this
was a sentiment that was common amongst people who had
gluten intolerances, and she was the constant symbol of that
for me. Thank you for sharing your trials and tribulations with
celiac disease and for being my guinea pig.
I love you more than I can say.

Table of Contents

Foreword

There are days in everyone's lives when someone says something that changes your life forever. If you are looking at this cookbook, you know the words . . . "You have Celiac Disease."

I was diagnosed in 1997 after blood tests and an endoscopy. I had no idea of just what that meant. I was told not to eat foods containing wheat, rye, barley, or oats. The wonderful thing was that all of a sudden I felt so much better. Those first days without bread, cake, or pasta were easy — and then I had to go shopping, and the real world set in.

I would look at ingredients without really knowing what I was looking for, so my diet became one of vegetables and protein. I found a few gluten-free items, but the taste really left much to be desired. I had to search in different stores that I had never frequented before. Some people knew about Celiac, but not very many.

As I had recently moved to a new area, I hadn't made new friends. When I went out to eat, I only had to speak to the wait person in an impersonal manner. After making friends, I found I had to explain, continually, about Celiac. Going to a new friend's home also became stressful. Everything was always about me and what I could eat. Now, everyone was patient and very nice, but I wanted to discuss other things besides my diet. I kept waiting for the day when it didn't come up, but I've discovered that never happens.

I wanted to invite my friends to my house, and at first I had to include foods that I would not touch or eat. I didn't know what to include for these dinners, and I certainly wanted my new friends to have a good time, but I always worried about wrongly ingesting something. It took lots of thought and preparation just for one meal.

In those early years, I made many mistakes. I remember one time in Vegas when visiting Monika and Jeff, I was in a casino. I felt my stomach churn and I was off running to the bathroom. I don't know how many people

I bumped into—I was too busy running to count.

It is so much easier now to find gluten-free food, and learning about what is gluten-free is so much easier, but I still fret about having people over, especially when they want to "bring something."

Now when I go out to dinner with friends and family, I don't have to say anything. Everyone chirps in with all the requirements. I do remember all those days, however, when it seemed like my life was turned upside down by the words . . . "You have Celiac Disease."

Roz Sudakow
(otherwise known as Mom)

Introduction

WHEN MY husband and I began dreaming about having a bed and breakfast/restaurant, we developed a concept of an old-fashioned country inn, where only one menu would be available nightly and the evening would be treated as a dinner party in a private home. These dinner parties would be themed by either a particular culture or a particular type of food, and the crowd would be limited to only five tables, one seating per night. When we began operating five years ago, the fixed price taster menu worked great, and only occasionally did we run into requests

for accommodations for food allergies or dietary restrictions. That has changed some. As time has gone on, we have noticed more and more requests for gluten-free menus. While I am unsure whether this phenomenon is a reflection of the increase in those with gluten intolerances or simply a reflection of the efficacy with which doctors are beginning to diagnose individuals with Celiac Disease or wheat allergies, the fact remains that we are seeing it more frequently. It is my mission to make sure these requests are met not just adequately but deliciously.

Take, for example, our annual New Year's Eve Party. For the last couple of years we have had one guest attend who has gluten intolerances. In a situation like this, with a large group attending an event, most of whom do not need to eat a gluten-free menu, I certainly do not want to make a completely different menu for one individual. At the same time I do not want the gluten-free individual to feel left out or have to worry about what they are eating. My solution has been to come up with a menu that just happens to be gluten-free, but that everyone else at the party will enjoy without any knowledge that there is anything out of the ordinary about the foods they are eating. I do so by selecting recipes using ingredients that are fresh and unprocessed, such as meats and vegetables, making sure my pantry is stocked with condiments and ingredients that are gluten-free, and making minor adjustments to items using flour by incorporating alternative gluten-free flours and nut meals which will not affect the texture or the taste of these recipes. Needless to say, the party is always a hit, people love the food, and nobody has any clue that they are eating a gluten-free menu by design.

So how do I know how to produce these gluten-free menus with confidence? This comes from not only my experiences over the years with gluten-free guests but also those with my mother-in-law, who was diagnosed with Celiac Disease in 1997. When she was first diagnosed, finding what she could and could not eat was extremely difficult. At the time ingredients were not particularly well labeled and there were not a lot of options for gluten-free products such as breads, pastas, and the like. We found that so many items we take for granted—like mayonnaise, soy sauce, sour cream, ketchup, and other condiments—were all potentially dangerous. It took quite a while to develop a proficiency at reading labels and identifying those ingredients that could pose problems.

Of course, with time, the day-to-day living part became easier, but there was still an issue with social situations. Restaurants were slow to catch on to the gluten-free wave, but many are beginning to develop gluten-free options that individuals can ask for. There is still a risk of cross-contamination, however, as many don't realize that even something simple like frying chicken and French fries in the same grease can cause a reaction. The bigger challenge, however, tends to be in either hosting or being invited to a party. While a professional chef in a restaurant may have a basic understanding of dietary restrictions because of their training, most amateur cooks—unless they are afflicted with or know anyone with gluten intolerances—are not aware of the pitfalls and dangers of the intolerance and are not certain how to adjust to cooking for them. What ends up happening to those with gluten intolerances, like my mother-in-law, is that they either bring their own food or end up eating before attending a social gathering to be sure they do not go hungry or inconvenience the host. And, to make matters worse, they end up spending their evening explaining why they cannot eat what everyone else is, taking all the fun out of the event. In some cases it is simply easier to decline an invitation then to have to deal with the hassle, and that just breaks my heart.

As far as I am concerned, one of the greatest pleasures in life is the social interaction one can experience through eating. I love food, I love talking about it, and to me nobody should be deprived of this pleasure simply because of food intolerances. Therefore, I felt compelled to write a cookbook enabling those with gluten intolerances and those who are hosting a party to which a person with gluten intolerances will be coming to make a menu that will be delicious and safe for everyone to eat. I wanted to take the guesswork out of being gluten-free and show that eating such a menu does not have to be boring or depriving. It can be just as flavorful, if not more so, because it takes advantage of largely fresh ingredients and minimizes the use of pre-packaged and processed foods.

To facilitate this process I have divided the book into sample theme parties, just as we do regularly here at the Chestnut Street Inn, and have listed recipes for each party within the section.

One thing I have learned from teaching cooking classes on the subject of cooking gluten-free is that once people have the basics and a guideline to go by, they feel empowered to branch out. Use these recipes as a baseline and expand on them. If you do not like mushrooms, leave them out. If you prefer something spicier or more acidic, adjust the recipe to your liking. The main thing is to know what pitfalls you can avoid, have specific brand names you can trust, and a general sense of where you can acquire most of the items you need to create these gluten-free recipes.

You will notice throughout the book that many of the recipes are Mediterranean in origin. As a cultural anthropologist with a focus on food, I lean toward cuisines of both the northern and southern Mediterranean. I have found that these cuisines naturally lend themselves to a gluten-free diet. They are rich in gluten-free spices and herbs and focus predominantly on locally available, seasonal produce and meat. While bread is a staple of many of the diets in this region, it is by no means the only thing consumed. I have found that when I provide enough diversity in a meal, most people do not miss the bread component and end up feeling perfectly satiated. And of course, you can always provide bread to those in attendance who are not on a gluten-free diet. Just be sure it is on a separate plate so as not to cross-contaminate any of the dishes.

I am a foodie in the greatest sense of the word. My dream was to take my hobby and passion for food and entertaining and to turn it into a career. I have been fortunate enough to do that. But it makes me sad to see people shy away from the joy of eating because of fear. I want everyone to be able to experience the pleasure of food with abandon, and that goes for those with gluten intolerances. If nothing else, I know that when my mother-in-law or other guests with gluten intolerances come to visit us at the inn, they are going to have a good time with food. If I can give them a way of taking that home and a few tools to help them achieve that sense of pleasure on their own, then I feel like I have accomplished something wonderful.

The Basics

How to read labels

The first step to cooking gluten-free is learning how to read labels. There are so many items in the store that are pre-packaged and processed. Many of these are laden with ingredients that are potentially dangerous for a gluten-free diet. Being aware of what these ingredients are and how to detect them is a key. Obviously anything with wheat, rye, barley, or oats is out. Oats in and of themselves are not a problem, but often oats are processed in the same mills as flour and therefore cross-contaminated. There are gluten-free oats now available that are processed in their own mills, but again, you have to double check the label. You should also be wary of items coming from foreign sources that have modified food starch and maltodextrin in them. While in the U.S. these ingredients are made with corn and rice derivatives, the same food and labeling standards are not necessarily practiced outside the country. My rule of thumb is if I cannot pronounce it, it probably is not safe. Simplistic? Perhaps, but effective. Better to err on the side of caution then to have a problem. And more and more labeling regulations are requiring items that are gluten- and wheat-free to be labeled clearly, thereby taking the guesswork out of the whole process.

How to stock a pantry

Spices. Next step to cooking gluten-free is stocking your pantry with ingredients that add flavor without adding gluten, namely spices. Spices are a key in my cooking. They are not only gluten-free in most cases (the one exception that comes to mind is Z'atar, which is a Middle Eastern spice that has wheat in it), but they are a wonderful way of keeping foods lower in fat and sugar. A triple whammy. I probably spend more time in my cooking classes educating people on spices and how to use them than anything else. It never ceases to amaze me how frightened people are about using and trying spices in their cooking. When they see me add a large quantity of cumin or paprika to something, I always hear an audible gasp which makes me laugh. "Why are you all so afraid of spices?" I ask. Usually I get an uncomfortable giggle and then we chat about it. I always reassure people that even when they think they have added enough spices to a dish, they could probably use more and it won't hurt a thing. When they begin to let go of their inhibitions, it amazes me how much joy they find in the discovery, like they have entered into a whole new world of culinary delight.

Keep in mind that you should rotate your spices every six months, so purchase them in smaller quantities and make sure you are getting them from a source that has not kept them on the store shelf for a long period of time. I tend to order mine from www. zamourispices.com, which is a Moroccan import store that happens to have an incredible selection of high quality spices, but other great sources are www.penzeys.com and www.thespicehouse.com. Many of the spices that will appear frequently in my recipes are Hungarian paprika, cumin, cinnamon, ginger, nutmeg, cloves, saffron and herbes de Provence, which is a spice blend from the Provence region of France that often contains thyme, tarragon, savory, chervil, and most importantly lavender. I try to avoid those containing rosemary as it tends to be too woody. Always keep your spices in an airtight container in a cool, dry place away from sunlight, and never refrigerate or freeze them.

Condiments. My third step to gluten-free cooking is to arm myself with oils, vinegars and other condiments that are gluten-free. I almost exclusively use extra virgin olive oil in both cooking and making dressings, but on occasion I also will use canola, vegetable, and argan oil. Argan is a specialty of Morocco that comes from the pit of the fruit of the argan tree, which only grows in the foothills of the Atlas Mountains. The pits are ground and then pressed to extract this delicious, nutty, and flavorful oil that can be used almost interchangeably with olive oil. Those who have potential peanut allergies may want to avoid the argan; although it has not been shown to cause reactions in people with nut allergies, it is essentially a tree nut. (Argan is available through www.zamourispices.com.) My favorite vinegars are good aged balsamic vinegars (read the label to be sure it is real balsamic vinegar and not wine vinegar to which coloring and other ingredients have been added) and various wine vinegars like pomegranate red wine vinegar and tarragon wine vinegar. These are fabulous for dressings and add a little hint of acidity to many dishes.

As for other condiments, some of the ones I use most frequently are pure maple syrup, Heinz ketchup, La Choy soy sauce, Grey Poupon Dijon mustard, honey, Lea & Perrins Worchestershire sauce and a North African chili paste called harissa. Harissa can be found at most international markets or online through www.zamourispices.com. Note: Brands are important here. Not all condiments are gluten-free. Be sure you have these brands on hand and again, if you are not sure, read the label.

Flours and Grains. Finally, keep beans, grains, nut meals, and flours on hand that are gluten-free. I always have a variety of both canned and dried beans, lentils, and peas around, which are great sources of fiber and protein. Rice, quinoa, some kasha, namely Wolff brand, and gluten-free corn and rice pastas are also great shelf-stable staples to have available. You'll find that the corn pastas or corn-and-rice pastas are so much like regular pasta that if you are using them in a recipe such as a pasta salad or bake of some kind, nobody will even know it is gluten-free. Pure rice pastas tend to be mushier and take longer to cook, so I generally stay away from them.

Quinoa is another wonderful grain because it is a pure source of protein and can really give you an extra punch of nutrition, not to mention it is delicious. I like to use it interchangeably with bulgur wheat for salads and sometimes instead of couscous as a side dish. It cooks just like rice and is becoming easier to find in standard grocery stores. Nut meals are my favorite thing to use not only for baking but as a substitute for bread crumbs in any kind of recipe. You can find almond, pecan, walnut, and hazelnut meals at most health food stores and even many grocery stores. They provide a wonderful contrast in texture in conjunction with gluten-free flours for baking, and they are a delicious crust for things like chicken or fish. They also happen to be lower in carbohydrates and sugars, so they are a good substitute for someone looking to cut carbohydrates whether for dietary purposes or diabetic purposes.

As far as gluten-free flours go, there are many available commercially now that you can buy pre-mixed rather than having to make your own all-purpose mix of tapioca, rice flour, potato starch, and xanthum gum, amongst other ingredients. My preferred brand is Domata Living Flour, which can be found at specialty retailers or online at www.domatalivingflour.com. It is recognized by the Celiac Sprue Association and bakes the most like regular all purpose flour. Other brands that I have used with fairly good results are Hodgson Mill and Bob's Red Mill, although I find that both of these yielded denser and more vegetable-flavored baked items. And apparently King Arthur is coming out with a new gluten-free all purpose flour, but I have yet to see it commercially available. A key to using these flours in baking is adding more moisture to help keep breads and pastries supple and combining them with cornmeal or nut meals to create a contrast in texture. Keep in mind, they will work much better in batters that use baking soda and baking powder for leavening such as quick breads than in yeast based breads, which rely on wheat gluten to develop their elasticity.

Shopping

More and more grocery stores now have gluten-free sections popping up. Even my local Walmart in rural Illinois has a large gluten-free section, much less other boutique and larger grocery chains in major metropolitan areas like Kroger and Hy-Vee. You can also request gluten-free products to be ordered by your local grocery chain if they do not carry a particular item you are looking for. Don't be afraid to ask! As long as they know they have a market to sell a product, they are usually more than happy to oblige. Finally, I highly recommend getting a good guide to gluten-free products, such as the most recent edition of the Celiac Sprue Association guide.

Some handy how-to tips —
balsamic reduction, 40
blow torch, using, 109
buttermilk,
    substitution for, 164
eggplant, choosing, 52
garlic, roasting, 106
jalapeños, roasting, 89
mushrooms, peeling, 47
peppers, roasting, 55
pomegranates, seeding, 133
lemons, preserving, 45
Tupperware, shaking, 103

And a few more interesting tidbits —
eggs, 166
fennel, 41
orange blossom water, 62
pastas, 70
ras el hanout, 44
saffron, 119
scallops, 27, 46
tahini paste, 51
wines for cooking, 104

Appetizer Party

APPETIZERS *are a wonderful way to entertain. I like them because most of the time once the party starts, you are done cooking and can really enjoy the party. It is also a casual and cost effective way to throw a party. Generally my rule of thumb for an appetizer party is to do six to seven dishes. I try to do two meat or seafood dishes, a dip or two, one other cold item, a cheese tray, and possibly a dessert. Below are a handful of savory items that work great together and just happen to be gluten-free.*

Monika's Mousse

Monika's Mousse is a four-layer terrine composed of layers of a sun-dried tomato paste, herbed goat cheese, homemade pesto, and a chicken mousse or pâté. It is a special recipe that grew out of a cooking battle my husband and I would have while living in Las Vegas. Based on the hit Food Network show Iron Chef, on our days off my husband would pick a theme ingredient for me to use and I would develop recipes based on these ingredients. This particular recipe came out of a chicken battle and is a great appetizer. You can serve it in individual slices with some gluten-free rice crackers and crudités or as a whole terrine on a plate surrounded by things to dip if you are hosting a buffet or cocktail party. Leftovers are great between two slices of bread for lunch, as the flavors develop the longer they are allowed to mingle in the refrigerator. This happens to be my mother-in-law's absolute favorite dish. Make sure you allow 24 hours for this one, as it has to set up or it won't hold together.

YIELDS APPROXIMATELY 12 SERVINGS

For the sun-dried tomato layer

½ cup sun-dried tomatoes
1 Tbsp minced garlic
Pinch kosher salt and
freshly ground pepper

2 Tbsp Daisy sour cream
¼ cup extra virgin olive
oil

Combine ingredients in a food processor and purée until a smooth paste is formed. Adjust seasonings to taste.

For the herbed goat cheese layer

4 oz fresh goat cheese,
softened
4 oz Philadelphia cream
cheese, softened
1 Tbsp minced garlic
3 Tbsp chopped assorted
fresh herbs (Italian

parsley, chives, and
basil are my favorite
combination, but use
any you like)
Pinch kosher salt and
freshly ground pepper

continued . . .

Place all the ingredients in a food processor and purée until the herbs are completely chopped and well incorporated into the cream cheese.

For the pesto layer

2 cups fresh basil leaves
½ cup toasted pine nuts
1 Tbsp minced garlic
Pinch kosher salt and
    freshly ground pepper

3 Tbsp lemon juice
¼ cup grated Parmesan
    cheese
¼-½ cup extra virgin
    olive oil

Combine ingredients except the olive oil in a food processor. Purée. Begin adding the olive oil slowly so the mix begins to emulsify or becomes thick and creamy. Adjust seasoning to taste.

For the chicken mousse layer

1 lb boneless, skinless
    chicken thighs
1 medium onion, diced
2 garlic cloves, minced
Kosher salt and freshly
    ground pepper
2 tsp Hungarian smoked
    hot paprika
¼-½ cup dry sherry

1 cup Kitchen Basics,
    Pacifica, or Progresso
    chicken broth
2 Tbsp extra virgin olive
    oil
2 Tbsp unsalted butter
1 tsp harissa
4 Tbsp Daisy sour cream

Place oil and butter in a large sauté pan over medium-high heat. When butter melts, add chicken pieces to the pan. Brown chicken evenly on both sides. Add onions to the pan and sauté for approximately 5 minutes until translucent. Add garlic and sauté for 1 minute until fragrant. Add spices and sauté for 1 minute to toast. Deglaze the pan with the sherry. Bring to a boil and cook uncovered until all the liquid has evaporated. Add chicken stock and bring to a boil. Reduce heat to a simmer and cover. Cook for approximately 45 minutes or until the chicken is tender. Remove the lid of the pan and return the pan to medium-high heat. Reduce liquid until almost all of it is gone. Continue stirring so as not to burn the chicken and the onions. Adjust seasoning to taste. Remove pan from heat and allow to cool completely. Add to a food processor along with the sour cream. Purée until the mixture is smooth and creamy. Adjust seasoning if needed and add more sour cream if the mix is too thick. The pâté should be creamy enough to spread on a piece of bread, like room-temperature peanut butter.

To assemble the terrine
Use a loaf pan lined with plastic wrap with enough overlap to eventually wrap over the terrine. Place the sun-dried tomato mixture on the bottom, spread in a thin layer. Top with the layer of herbed cream cheese, followed by the pesto. The last layer is the chicken mousse. Once the layers are placed in the pan, fold the edges of plastic wrap around the terrine, making sure it is well covered. If there are any gaps, use additional plastic wrap to secure the terrine in the pan. Place in the refrigerator, weighed down by either a few cans or a box of stock. The mousse should set for at least 8 hours, but is best after 24 hours. To serve, turn the terrine out of the loaf pan and unwrap the plastic. Carefully slice the terrine into ½" slices and arrange lying on its side on a plate so that the colors of the layers show nicely. Serve with gluten-free rice crackers and crudités. Or turn out entire loaf onto a serving plate and serve on a buffet with nut thins and crudités.

Hungarian-Style Deviled Eggs (Casino Eggs)

My grandma invented these eggs. While I'm not sure why she called them "Casino" Eggs, a guest who recently enjoyed them here at the inn said it is like a casino because when you eat them, you hit the jackpot. I love that.

YIELDS 12 APPETIZER PORTIONS

12 eggs
2 Tbsp unsalted butter
1 Tbsp extra virgin olive oil
Kosher salt and freshly ground pepper
Pinch freshly grated nutmeg
2 tsp herbes de Provence
¼ cup dry sherry or dry vermouth
16 oz sliced mushrooms
2 shallots, sliced

2-3 garlic cloves, minced
8 Tbsp Hellmans mayonnaise
4 Tbsp Daisy sour cream
Juice of ½ lemon
1 tsp Grey Poupon Dijon mustard
1 tsp anchovy paste
1 garlic clove, minced
Pinch Hungarian hot paprika
Pinch chopped Italian parsley

Place eggs in plenty of cold salted water. Bring to a boil and cook 10 minutes. Remove from heat and rinse under cold water. Let cool and peel. Cut eggs in half and pop yolks out into a bowl. Add oil and butter to a medium sauté pan and heat over medium-high heat until butter is melted and bubbling. Add shallots and sauté for a couple of minutes until they begin to caramelize. Add garlic and sauté for 1 minute or until fragrant. Add mushrooms and season with salt, pepper, nutmeg, and herbes de Provence. Deglaze the pan with sherry or vermouth and cook on high until all the liquid has evaporated and the mushrooms begin to caramelize. Cool completely. Combine mushrooms with 2 Tbsp mayonnaise and 1 Tbsp sour cream. Adjust seasoning to taste. Coat the bottom of serving dish with mushroom mixture.

Combine egg yolks with 2 Tbsp mayonnaise, 1 Tbsp mustard, anchovy paste, garlic, salt, and pepper. Fill each egg half with yolk filling and place filling side down on the mushrooms. Combine 4 Tbsp mayonnaise with 2 Tbsp sour cream, 1 Tbsp sugar, lemon juice, salt, and pepper. Pour dressing over the eggs, coating completely. Sprinkle with paprika and chopped parsley to garnish. Serve well chilled.

Caramelized Onion and Garlic Dip

Make plenty of this one. The leftovers are great on sandwiches.

Yields 8-10 Servings

1 red onion, sliced
2 leeks, finely sliced
2-3 garlic cloves, minced
2 Tbsp olive oil
1 Tbsp unsalted butter
Pinch kosher salt and
*   freshly ground pepper*
Pinch Hungarian hot
*   paprika*

2 tsp harissa
8 oz Philadelphia
*   cream cheese, room*
*   temperature*
½ cup Daisy sour cream
¾ cup Hellmans
*   mayonnaise*

Heat the olive oil and butter in a medium sauté pan over medium-high heat until the butter has melted and is bubbling. Add onion and leek and season with salt, pepper, and paprika. Reduce heat to low and sauté over low heat for approximately 20 minutes or until the onions are brown and caramelized. Add garlic and sauté for an additional minute. Remove from heat and allow to cool. Transfer to a food processor and add cream cheese, sour cream, and mayonnaise. Purée on high until smooth and creamy. Season to taste. Serve with nut thins and crudités.

Crab Cakes with Remoulade Sauce

Everyone loves a good crab cake, but what I can't stand is a crab cake that is more cake than crab. These cakes use little "breading," in the form of pecan or almond meal, which keeps them light and delicious.

YIELDS 8 SERVINGS—2 PER PERSON

1 lb canned lump crab
   meat, drained
¼ to ½ cup plus ¾ to 1 cup
   almond or pecan meal
2 eggs
1 Tbsp Grey Poupon
   Dijon mustard
1 tsp Lea & Perrins
   Worcestershire sauce
2 Tbsp chopped Italian
   parsley

2 Tbsp chopped cilantro
3-4 scallions, diced
2 Tbsp lemon juice
1 tsp Old Bay seasoning
½ cup Hellmans
   mayonnaise
1 tsp minced garlic
Pinch kosher salt and
   freshly ground pepper
¼-½ cup extra virgin
   olive oil

For the cakes, combine crab with eggs, mustard, Worcestershire sauce, parsley, cilantro, scallions, Old Bay seasoning, lemon juice, mayonnaise, garlic, and enough almond or pecan meal to just hold the cakes together but not make them too doughy. Using your hands, gently work mixture until all the ingredients are combined well. Don't overmix. Place remaining nut meal in a bowl. Form mixture into approximately 1" diameter cakes, coating them lightly with almond or pecan meal before placing them on a baking sheet. Once all the cakes are formed, place baking sheet in a refrigerator for at least 30 minutes before frying.

Heat olive oil in a medium sauté pan over medium-high heat until the oil spatters when sprinkled with water. Place cakes in hot oil and brown evenly on both sides, approximately 3 minutes per side. Transfer to a baking sheet lined with paper towels and place in an oven set on low until ready to serve. Serve hot with remoulade sauce.

For the sauce

1 cup Hellmans
  mayonnaise
1 Tbsp chopped Bubbie's
  dill pickles
2 tsp Grey Poupon Dijon
  mustard
2 Tbsp minced Italian
  parsley

2 Tbsp minced cilantro
2 scallions, minced
2 Tbsp lemon juice
Pinch kosher salt and
  freshly ground pepper
1 Tbsp chopped capers
1 tsp harissa

Combine all the ingredients and whisk together. Place in a refrigerator for at least an hour to allow the flavors to develop.

Bacon-Wrapped Scallops with Honey Dijon BBQ Sauce

Normally scallops are a challenge to cook because they go from delicious to rubber in seconds. However, wrapped in bacon, they stay moist, and this takes most of the guesswork out of cooking them. If you prefer shrimp, you can do the exact same recipe with peeled and deveined shrimp.

YIELDS 12 SERVINGS—2 PER PERSON

24 medium-sized scallops
12 slices bacon

Preheat the broiler. Cut bacon slices in half. Wrap each scallop in a half slice of bacon and secure with a toothpick. Place on an ungreased baking sheet with a lip. Broil approximately 5 minutes per side or until the bacon is crispy. Serve hot with sauce.

For the sauce

½ cup Heinz ketchup
¼ cup water
⅛ cup balsamic vinegar
⅛ cup chopped shallots
1 Tbsp honey
1 tsp Lea & Perrins
  Worcestershire sauce
Pinch kosher salt

Pinch freshly ground
  pepper
1 Tbsp Grey Poupon
  Dijon mustard
1 tsp garlic powder
1 Tbsp harissa or pinch
  of crushed red pepper
  flakes

Place all the ingredients in a saucepan. Bring to a boil and then reduce heat to a simmer. Simmer for approximately 10 minutes, stirring occasionally, until the sauce has reduced and thickened.

Here is another combination of appetizers that are great for a party. Feel free to mix and match. That's part of the fun.

Hungarian Paprika Dip

This is another recipe handed down from my grandma. We always had this on the table whenever there was a family gathering for as long as I can remember. It is a simple yet delicious dip that is unusual enough that it'll be a surprise to all your guests.

YIELDS APPROXIMATELY 10 SERVINGS

3 8-oz packages
  Philadelphia cream
  cheese, softened
1 stick unsalted butter,
  softened
2 Tbsp Daisy sour cream
4-6 scallions, chopped
2 Tbsp Grey Poupon
  Dijon mustard
2-3 garlic cloves, minced
2-3 Tbsp Hungarian
  smoked hot paprika

Pinch kosher salt and
  freshly ground pepper
1 tsp anchovy paste
  (Do not leave this out.
  It is a key flavoring
  that will make or break
  the dish. Don't worry,
  it won't taste fishy
  at all. It simply adds
  a depth of flavor and
  saltiness unlike any
  other in the world.)

Place all the ingredients into a food processor and purée. Season to taste. Dip should be bright orange. If it is too pale, add more paprika to enhance the color. Serve with and crudités.

Sausage-Stuffed Mushrooms

These sausage-stuffed mushrooms are lighter than typical as they do not use any bread crumbs, which of course is ideal for a gluten-free menu. They are also one of our most popular appetizers at the inn.

YIELDS 12 SERVINGS

24 stuffer mushrooms, stems removed, peeled (see p. 48)
¼ cup dry vermouth or dry sherry
1 lb bulk sausage
1 Tbsp Italian seasoning or herbes de Provence
1 8-oz package Philadelphia cream cheese, softened
1 tsp Lea & Perrins Worcestershire sauce

½ cup grated Parmesan cheese plus 2-3 Tbsp for sprinkling over top of mushrooms
Pinch kosher salt and freshly ground pepper
2 tsp garlic powder
Pinch freshly grated nutmeg
1 egg
2 tsp white truffle oil (optional)

Begin by browning the sausage with Italian seasoning or herbes de Provence in a medium sauté pan over medium-high heat for approximately 10 minutes or until no pink remains. If the sausage is very fatty, drain before assembling. If the sausage is only a little fatty, keep the fat as it will keep the mushrooms moist. Cool filling completely before assembling mushrooms.

Preheat oven to 375 degrees. Place mushrooms on a baking sheet and drizzle with vermouth or sherry. Combine sausage with cream cheese, Worcestershire sauce, Parmesan, salt, pepper, garlic powder, nutmeg, and egg. Make sure filling is well combined. It is easiest to use your hands for this process. Fill each mushroom cap with approximately 1 Tbsp filling until all filling has been used. Sprinkle with more grated Parmesan and drizzle with truffle oil if using. Bake approximately 15 minutes or until tops begin to turn golden. Serve hot.

Spinach and Artichoke Dip

I love spinach and artichoke dip but am often hesitant to order it because there is a lot of flour in it as a binder. This version uses cornstarch as a thickener, which doesn't change the flavor any and of course makes it gluten-free. Herbes de Provence is a French spice blend that generally contains thyme, savory, chervil, tarragon, and lavender. I use it a lot in my cooking, as you will see throughout this book. Be sure to buy one that has the lavender in it. I tend to avoid those that also contain rosemary, as I find it to be overpowering.

YIELDS APPROXIMATELY 8 SERVINGS

1 lb fresh baby spinach leaves
4 shallots, sliced
3-4 garlic cloves, minced
2 cans artichoke hearts, drained and chopped
2 Tbsp unsalted butter
2 Tbsp extra virgin olive oil

Kosher salt and freshly ground pepper
Pinch freshly grated nutmeg
2 tsp herbes de Provence
2 tsp cornstarch, dissolved in 2 Tbsp water
2 cups heavy cream
2 cups shredded Gruyère or Asiago

Heat oil and butter in a medium saucepan over medium-high heat until the butter has melted and is bubbling. Add shallots and sauté until just golden. Add garlic and sauté an additional minute or until fragrant. Add spinach and artichokes. Season with salt, pepper, nutmeg, and herbes de Provence. Continue to sauté until the spinach has wilted down and most of the liquid has evaporated, approximately 5 minutes. Add heavy cream and dissolved cornstarch and heat through until thickened. Add cheese and continue cooking until the cheese has melted thoroughly. Adjust seasoning to taste. Serve hot with crudités and nut thins, which are readily available at most grocery stores and are delicious.

Meatballs (Albóndigas) in Spicy Tomato Chocolate Sauce

Another recipe I first served for one of our chocolate extravaganzas. This one is really unusual and will certainly be more fun to serve than a traditional Swedish meatball, which to me is boring and greasy.

YIELDS APPROXIMATELY 12 SERVINGS

For the meatballs

1 lb ground beef
1 ½ lb ground pork
1 cup almond meal
2-3 garlic cloves, minced
3-4 shallots, minced
2 Tbsp chopped cilantro
2 Tbsp chopped parsley
1 Tbsp dried oregano
2 tsp kosher salt

1 tsp freshly ground pepper
Pinch cayenne pepper
½ tsp ground allspice
1 tsp ground coriander
1 tsp ground cinnamon
2 eggs, beaten
2-3 Tbsp vegetable oil

Combine all ingredients except the oil in a large mixing bowl and knead by hand until all the ingredients are well combined. Roll the mixture into 1" meatballs and refrigerate 30 minutes. Heat oil in a large sauté pan and brown the meatballs on all sides. Remove from the pan. Set aside in the refrigerator while making the sauce.

For the sauce

2 28-oz cans whole peeled
  tomatoes, crushed by
  hand
1 medium red onion,
  chopped
2-3 garlic cloves, minced
1 tsp ground cinnamon
½ tsp ground allspice
1 tsp ground coriander

1 tsp dried oregano
Pinch kosher salt and
  freshly ground pepper
2-3 chopped chipotle
  peppers in adobo sauce
4 oz bittersweet chocolate
1-2 Tbsp sugar or honey
½-1 cup Kitchen Basics,
  Pacifica, or Progresso
  chicken broth

In the same sauté pan used to brown meatballs, add onion and sauté approximately 5 minutes or until the onions are translucent. Add garlic and cook for 1 minute or until fragrant. Add cinnamon, allspice, coriander, oregano, salt, and pepper. Cook an additional minute to toast the spices. Add crushed tomatoes and chipotle pepper with adobo sauce. Bring to a boil. Simmer on low heat, uncovered, for approximately an hour or until the sauce has thickened, stirring occasionally so as not to burn the sauce. Using an immersion blender, purée the sauce until it is nice and creamy. Add chocolate and stir over low heat until melted. Add chicken broth and sugar or honey as needed. Adjust seasoning to taste. Return meatballs to sauce and cook on medium heat for approximately 10 minutes. Serve hot.

Green Eggs and Ham

Inspired by the classic Dr. Seuss book, this recipe is great for a cocktail party. It is a crowd pleaser and a good conversation piece. A reminder: it cannot be made too far in advance as the avocado will oxidize and turn brown.

Yields Approximately 12 Servings

12 eggs
1 avocado, peeled, seeded
  and diced
1 cup fresh herbs (Italian
  parsley, basil, and
  chives are a good
  combo)
2 garlic cloves
4 Tbsp Daisy sour cream

2 Tbsp Grey Poupon
  Dijon mustard
Pinch kosher salt and
  freshly ground pepper
1 Tbsp lemon juice
2 Tbsp Hellmanns
  mayonnaise
3 slices cooked applewood
  smoked bacon, crumbled

Place the eggs in a saucepan. Cover with cold water and a pinch of salt. Bring to a boil. Cook the eggs approximately 10 minutes. Remove from heat and run cold water over the eggs to stop the cooking process. Once cooled, peel the eggs and cut them in half, removing the yolks carefully without tearing the egg whites. Combine half of the yolks with the avocado, herbs, garlic, sour cream, salt and pepper, mustard, lemon juice, and mayonnaise in the bowl of a food processor. Blend until the mixture forms a smooth paste. Place the filling into a Ziploc baggie. Cut a small hole in the bottom corner of the baggie and pipe the mixture into the prepared egg whites. Top each egg with a piece of crumbled bacon. Serve immediately.

Spanish Tapas

T he word "tapas" is used colloquially as "little dishes." These little dishes of love are a wonderful way to entertain. You get a sampling of many dishes rather than one main course, and it is a communal style of dining that lends itself to a party.

Sangria would of course be the drink of choice here. An easy way to make a good sangria is to use a bottle of good red Spanish wine like a Rioja, mix with a couple of cups of orange juice, and then cut up a bunch of fresh fruit and soak it in the wine mixture overnight. Serve chilled with a disclaimer that the fruit is going to be really potent—so be careful about eating too much of it unless not remembering the party is something that sounds appealing to you.

Campari Tomatoes Stuffed with Goat Cheese and Tapenade

This is my personal favorite. It's simple, yet delicious. The contrast of the acidity of the tomato with the creamy tang of the goat cheese and the saltiness of the tapenade is just perfect.

YIELDS 6 SERVINGS

12 Campari tomatoes
4 oz fresh goat cheese

For the tapenade
12 pitted Spanish olives
3 Tbsp capers
6 Tbsp Hellmans mayonnaise
2-3 garlic cloves, minced
2-3 Tbsp Italian parsley, chopped

Cut a thin slice off bottom of tomatoes to make them flat. Then cut the top of the tomatoes off and scoop out the seeds using a paring knife. Mince olives and capers. Combine with mayonnaise, garlic, and parsley. Place small amount of goat cheese in each tomato. Then add tapenade mix on top of goat cheese. Serve chilled with balsamic reduction .

Balsamic Reduction

This is a garnish I keep on hand for everything. The balsamic becomes very sweet after reducing and not only looks beautiful on the plate but is a great contrast of flavor with almost anything, particularly fatty dishes.

1 bottle of balsamic vinegar. (Make sure you read your label. Some "balsamic vinegars" are actually wine vinegar that has been dyed and flavored to mimic authentic balsamic vinegar.)

Place contents of the bottle in a small saucepan and bring to a boil. Reduce to a simmer and allow to reduce until only about ⅓ of the liquid remains. Store at room temperature in a squirt bottle for future use. This has an unlimited shelf life, although it won't last that long.

Orange and Fennel Salad

Most people aren't familiar with fennel. It is a delicious root from a plant with fronds that look a lot like dill. The flavor is licorice, and it gives a wonderful fresh flavor to any salad. Fennel roots are also delicious roasted as a side dish. When shopping for them, look for ones that are firm and have a clear white flesh. If you notice the bulb is beginning to get orange stripes on it that almost look like rust, it is past its prime.

YIELDS 6-8 SERVINGS

4 navel oranges or blood oranges
1 fennel bulb, quartered, and sliced, and fennel fronds reserved for garnish
1 red onion, sliced
2-3 garlic cloves, minced
2 Tbsp extra virgin olive oil or argan oil
Handful Spanish olives

1 tsp Hungarian smoked hot paprika
1 red chili pepper, seeded and chopped
¼ cup Italian parsley, chopped
Kosher salt and freshly ground pepper
2-3 Tbsp orange blossom water

Grate rind of all the oranges with a micro plane and reserve. Cut off both ends of each orange and peel oranges. Cut into segments, reserving any juice that comes out for the dressing. Toss fennel, red onion, garlic, orange segments, chili pepper, and olives together. Season with paprika, salt, and pepper. Drizzle oil, orange blossom water, and reserved orange juice over the salad. Garnish with orange rind, parsley, and reserved fennel fronds.

Tuna and Rice Salad

This salad is the one amongst all the Spanish Tapas that causes people to give us the old stink eye. But it is one that always surprises and ends up being a crowd favorite. My husband adores it, and so I couldn't have had a Spanish tapas menu without it. For a nice alternative, use canned salmon. It gives it an almost meatier, heartier texture. You can either use jarred roasted red peppers or if you would like, you can roast them yourself over an open gas flame or in the oven.

YIELDS APPROXIMATELY 8 SERVINGS

2 Tbsp extra virgin olive oil
1 cup long grain rice
2 cups Kitchen Basics, Pacifica, or Progresso chicken broth
½ tsp herbes de Provence
Pinch kosher salt and freshly ground pepper
1 5-oz can tuna in water, drained and flaked
2 Tbsp Italian parsley, minced
2 Tbsp roasted pepper (see p. 87), minced
2-3 garlic cloves, minced
1 cup Hellmans mayonnaise
6 Tbsp Heinz ketchup
½ tsp Lea & Perrins Worcestershire sauce
1 tsp red wine vinegar

Place olive oil, rice, chicken broth, herbes de Provence, salt, and pepper in a medium saucepan. Bring to a boil and cover. Reduce to a simmer and cook for approximately 18-20 minutes or until the rice is cooked. Fluff rice when done and add the tuna, parsley, roasted peppers, and garlic. Combine mayo, ketchup, Worcestershire sauce, red wine vinegar, and a pinch of salt and pepper to taste in a small bowl. Toss rice in dressing and serve immediately or allow to sit in the refrigerator to marinate until ready to serve.

Paprika Pork Ribs

Choose bone-in ribs for this. While you won't get as much meat as you would with boneless, the bone actually imparts a wonderful flavor upon the pork as it simmers away. Plus it's kind of fun to eat them. There's no way to do it without using your fingers and making a mess, so make sure to provide plenty of napkins.

YIELDS 6-8 SERVINGS

1 Tbsp olive oil	2 tsp Hungarian hot
2 lbs pork spare ribs	paprika
1 red onion, diced	1 Tbsp harissa
Pinch kosher salt and	1 cup dry vermouth or dry
freshly ground pepper	sherry
2 tsp dried oregano	8 garlic cloves, peeled
1 bay leaf	1 cup chicken broth

Combine all the ingredients and marinate for at least an hour or overnight. Place in a large stockpot and bring to a boil. Cover and reduce to a simmer. Simmer for approximately 1 hour or until the ribs are tender. Remove lid and bring to a boil. Continue cooking until most of the liquid has evaporated and thickened.

Garlic Shrimp

This recipe has a little bit of a Moroccan influence. Spain and Morocco share a long history together—not only the Moorish architecture but the flavors which have passed back and forth, thanks to the Spanish occupation of parts of Morocco and the daily ferry which crosses the Straits of Gibraltar between the two countries.

YIELDS APPROXIMATELY 6 SERVINGS

1 lb shrimp, peeled and deveined
Kosher salt and freshly ground pepper
2-3 tsp ras el hanout*
3-4 garlic cloves, minced
3 Tbsp unsalted butter
2 Tbsp extra virgin olive oil
2 tsp harissa or pinch of of crushed red pepper flakes

1 preserved lemon, peel only, rinsed and chopped (can be purchased through zamourispices.com or you can make them yourself)
3-4 Tbsp lemon juice
2 Tbsp cilantro, chopped
2 Tbsp Italian parsley, chopped

Toss shrimp with salt, pepper, and ras el hanout to coat evenly. Heat oil and butter in a large sauté pan over medium-high heat. Add garlic and harissa or pepper flakes and sauté for 1 minute or until fragrant. Add shrimp and allow to set for approximately 2 minutes in a single layer. Turn over and continue cooking an additional 2-3 minutes or until the shrimp are curled into a tight "C" and pink. Add lemon juice, preserved lemon peel, cilantro, and parsley. Toss to coat and serve immediately.

* Ras el hanout: Moroccan spice blend literally translated to "Top of the Shop." Can have up to 40 different spices in it.

Preserved Lemons

I keep a large batch of these going at all times so it is always on hand.

1 medium Mason jar
Kosher salt
4-6 lemons

Lemon juice to cover (use
ReaLemon if lemons
aren't particularly juicy.)

Cut lemons in quarters, keeping one end attached. Stuff full of kosher salt and fit as many lemons as you can into the jar tightly. Cover with lemon juice and seal. Place in a cool, dry place away from sunlight for 6 weeks to preserve. To use, throw away fruit and rinse peel. Chop and throw into salads, soups, stews, or anywhere the recipe calls for lemon zest. Preserved lemons will keep for up to a year at room temperature in a cool, dry place.

Saffron Scallops

This recipe uses sea scallops, which are larger and meatier than bay scallops. They are sometimes a challenge to find, so if you can't find them, go ahead and use bay scallops. You won't get quite the browning on the scallops, but the flavor will be just as good.

YIELDS APPROXIMATELY 8-10 SERVINGS

2 Tbsp olive oil
1 Tbsp unsalted butter
2 shallots, sliced
2 garlic cloves, minced
Pinch kosher salt and freshly ground pepper
Pinch Hungarian hot paprika
Pinch saffron

1 lb sea scallops, patted dry with a paper towel
2 oz Canadian bacon, diced
2 Tbsp dry vermouth or dry sherry
2 Tbsp Italian parsley, chopped

Season the scallops with salt, pepper, and paprika. Heat olive oil and butter in a medium sauté pan over medium-high heat. Add Canadian bacon and sauté until the bacon is crisp and begins to turn golden. Add shallots and sauté for a minute or until the shallots begin to caramelize. Add garlic and sauté for a minute or until just fragrant. Add saffron and heat through to release some of the color. Add scallops and sear on first side for approximately 3 minutes or until they turn golden. Turn over. Add vermouth or sherry and continue cooking an additional 2-3 minutes or until the scallops have just cooked through and some of the liquid has evaporated. Add parsley at the very last minute and serve hot.

Garlic Sautéed Mushrooms

Whenever I teach cooking classes and tell people to peel their mushrooms I get perplexed looks. Mushrooms are generally grown in horse manure and are therefore pretty dirty little guys. They are also made up largely of water, and you never want to wash them or they will become water-logged and spongy. So there remains the issue of cleaning them. You can wipe them gently with a damp cloth or you can peel them. Simply pop the stems out and remove them. They are usually pretty chewy and not my favorite thing to eat anyway. After you remove the stem you'll notice a flap on the inside of the mushroom. If you grab the flap, you can easily peel away the skin of the mushroom, leaving a clean mushroom behind. This will also have the added bonus of giving the mushroom a better texture by eliminating one layer of the chewiness that often makes people not like the texture of mushrooms.

YIELDS 6-8 SERVINGS

1 lb small mushrooms, stems removed and peeled
4 garlic cloves, minced
3 shallots, sliced
Kosher salt and freshly ground pepper
Pinch freshly grated nutmeg
3 tsp herbes de Provence
2 Tbsp unsalted butter
2 Tbsp extra virgin olive oil
½ cup dry sherry

Heat oil and butter in a medium sauté pan over medium-high heat. Add shallots and sauté for a couple of minutes until they begin to turn golden. Add garlic and sauté for 1 minute or until fragrant. Add mushrooms, salt, pepper, nutmeg, and herbes de Provence. Sauté for 1 minute to toast the herbs. Add sherry and bring to a boil. Continue cooking on high until all the liquid has evaporated and the mushrooms begin to caramelize. Adjust seasoning to taste and serve hot.

Roasted Potatoes and Pearl Onions

If you can't find fingerling potatoes, use any small roasting potato. Fingerlings just have a marvelous buttery flavor and unique tender texture when roasted. If possible, buy pre-peeled pearl onions in the freezer section of your grocery store. They are a pain to peel. If you cannot find them already peeled, simply cover the onions with boiling water for approximately 1 minute and then drain. The peels should come off fairly easily after that.

YIELDS APPROXIMATELY 8 SERVINGS

1 lb fingerling potatoes
1 lb pearl onions, peeled
1 head garlic, cloves
   removed and peeled
2 Tbsp herbes de Provence

1 Tbsp Hungarian smoked
   hot paprika
Kosher salt and freshly
   ground pepper
3-4 Tbsp extra virgin
   olive oil

Place potatoes, onions, and garlic on a baking sheet. Drizzle with olive oil and season liberally with salt and pepper. Then sprinkle herbes de Provence and paprika over them and toss gently to coat, spreading them out into one layer so they roast evenly. Place in a preheated 375 degree oven for approximately 45 minutes until the potatoes are golden and tender. Serve hot.

Homemade Cinnamon Ice Cream

Ice cream isn't very hard to make, it just takes some time if you don't own an ice cream machine. Keep in mind, there are a number of ice creams that are not gluten-free, so if you can take the time to make your own, it is definitely worth the effort.

Yields 6-8 Servings

6 egg yolks
1⅓ cups granulated sugar
2½ cups heavy cream

1 tsp pure vanilla extract
2-3 tsp ground cinnamon

Whisk egg yolks and sugar until pale and creamy. Heat cream in a medium saucepan over medium to medium-low heat until small bubbles begin to form around the edges of the saucepan. Remove from heat. Slowly whisk hot cream into egg mixture, whisking constantly so as not to scramble the eggs. Pour egg/cream mixture back into the saucepan and place over low heat, stirring constantly with a wooden spoon until the mixture thickens enough to coat the back of the spoon, but not enough to curdle the eggs. Remove from heat and pour through a sieve into a metal bowl that has been placed in an ice bath. Stir in vanilla and cinnamon and allow to cool completely. Cover tightly with plastic wrap and place in the freezer overnight to set. Alternately, pour into an ice cream machine and freeze according to manufacturer's directions. Transfer into a Tupperware container and place in the freezer for storage. Remove from the freezer a few minutes before serving.

Middle Eastern Mezze

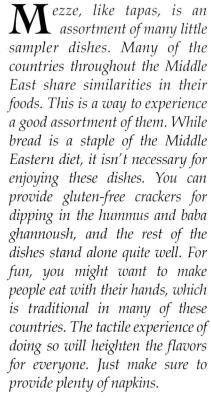

Mezze, like tapas, is an assortment of many little sampler dishes. Many of the countries throughout the Middle East share similarities in their foods. This is a way to experience a good assortment of them. While bread is a staple of the Middle Eastern diet, it isn't necessary for enjoying these dishes. You can provide gluten-free crackers for dipping in the hummus and baba ghannoush, and the rest of the dishes stand alone quite well. For fun, you might want to make people eat with their hands, which is traditional in many of these countries. The tactile experience of doing so will heighten the flavors for everyone. Just make sure to provide plenty of napkins.

To complete the meal, get some Moroccan mint tea bags from Stash Teas. You can steep them in hot water. Cool. Then mix with sugar and pour over ice for a fantastic iced mint tea. Or, if you are feeling really adventuresome, you can order a blend of Moroccan mint tea and dried mint from www.zamourispices.com and brew that as a special treat. Remember to add plenty of sugar to it. They like their tea sweet.

Hummus bi Tahina

I always joke with my friends that if there were only one food left on the planet for me or if I were stuck on a deserted island, I would want to have a big bowl of hummus to eat. To me it is the perfect food. High in fiber, protein, and good fats—and of course delicious. Don't skip peeling the chickpeas. This is the key to a creamy versus grainy hummus.

Tahini paste, which is a sesame paste, is usually found in the section of the grocery store where you find peanut butter. I prefer imported tahinis over domestic ones, which tend to be very thick and more difficult to incorporate. Store tahini at room temperature and shake well before use.

YIELDS 8 SERVINGS

2 cans chickpeas, drained
¼ cup tahini paste
2 Tbsp lemon juice
Pinch kosher salt and
    freshly ground pepper
1 tsp Hungarian hot
    paprika

1 tsp ground cumin
1 tsp harissa or pinch of
    cayenne pepper
3-4 crushed garlic cloves
¼ cup olive oil
¼–½ cup water

Soak chickpeas in water for approximately 1 hour. Using your fingers, peel the outer layer of skin off each chickpea before transferring them to the bowl of a food processor. Add tahini paste, lemon juice, salt, pepper, cumin, paprika, harissa or cayenne, garlic, and olive oil to chickpeas and process in a food processor until the mix is smooth. Slowly add water to thin the hummus until it becomes creamy and easily spreadable. Adjust seasoning to taste. Serve sprinkled with paprika and drizzled with olive oil, accompanied with some good imported olives. (You can order several kinds of olives from www.zamourispices. com, or many grocery stores now have olive bars that are well stocked with olives from all over the world.)

Baba Ghannoush

The key to a good baba ghannoush is to find good eggplants. You want eggplants without too many seeds. How do you tell this without cutting them open? Tap them. If they sound hollow, they have a lot of seeds; if they sound solid, they don't. You should also look for eggplants that have a firm, black flesh without many blemishes.

YIELDS APPROXIMATELY 8 SERVINGS

2 globe eggplants
3 garlic cloves, peeled
1 tsp ground cumin
1 tsp Hungarian hot
    paprika
2 tsp harissa or pinch
    of crushed red pepper
    flakes

Pinch kosher salt and
    freshly ground pepper
⅓ cup lemon juice
½ cup tahini paste
⅓ cup extra virgin olive
    oil
1 Tbsp Italian parsley,
    chopped

Preheat oven to 350 degrees. Prick the eggplants several times with a fork. Place them on a baking sheet and roast for approximately 45 minutes to an hour, rotating periodically to ensure they roast evenly. Remove from the oven and allow the eggplants to cool completely. Peel eggplants and chop up the meat. Place in a food processor along with garlic, cumin, paprika, salt, pepper, harissa or pepper flakes, lemon juice, tahini, and olive oil. Purée until smooth. Adjust seasoning to taste. Serve at room temperature, drizzled with olive oil and sprinkled with parsley and paprika. Garnish with olives.

Quinoa Salad Tabbouli Style

Tabbouli or bulgur wheat salad is one of the most traditional salads in the Middle East, but obviously it isn't gluten-free. In looking for alternatives to the bulgur I happened upon quinoa, which is being touted as a new super food. A relative of spinach and tumbleweed, quinoa is a South American grain that cooks exactly like rice, looks like a cross between bulgur and couscous, and is unlike anything else. It is a perfect grain for salads, soups, or side dishes and is ideal for gluten-free, vegetarian, or vegan diets because it is a nutritional powerhouse with more protein than most meats. So eat up!

YIELDS APPROXIMATELY 8 SERVINGS

For the salad
- 1 cup quinoa
- 2 cups water
- 1 cup grape tomatoes, halved
- 1 English cucumber, peeled and chopped
- 4 scallions, chopped
- 3-4 garlic cloves, minced
- 1 bunch Italian parsley, chopped
- 1 bunch cilantro, chopped
- Handful fresh mint, chopped

For the dressing
- ⅓ cup lemon juice
- ¼ cup extra virgin olive oil
- Kosher salt and freshly ground pepper
- 1 tsp ground cumin
- 1 tsp Hungarian hot paprika

Cook quinoa as you do rice: 2 to 1 ratio for approximately 18 minutes. Using a fork, lightly fluff the quinoa and then spread out in a thin layer on a baking sheet. Allow to dry for an additional hour before using. Add tomatoes, cucumber, scallions, garlic, parsley, cilantro, and mint to quinoa.

To prepare dressing, whisk lemon juice and olive oil along with the salt, pepper, cumin, and paprika until well combined. Pour over the quinoa and vegetables and toss gently to mix. Allow to marinate for at least an hour in the refrigerator. This salad tastes better after marinating 24 hours.

Lamb Köfte with Tomato Coulis

Köfte are basically ground meat kebabs. They can be made with lamb, beef or chicken and are very traditional street foods in North Africa and the Middle East.

YIELDS 4 SERVINGS

For the köfte
- 1 lb ground lamb
- Pinch kosher salt and freshly ground pepper
- 1 tsp ground cumin
- 1 tsp Hungarian hot paprika
- ½ tsp ground coriander
- 1 tsp garlic powder

For the coulis
- 2 Vidalia onions, minced
- 2-3 garlic cloves, minced
- 1 28-oz can fire-roasted diced tomatoes
- 2-3 Tbsp argan oil
- Pinch kosher salt and freshly ground pepper
- 1 tsp ground cumin
- 1 tsp Hungarian hot paprika
- ½ tsp ground coriander
- 1 tsp harissa
- 2 Tbsp honey

Combine lamb with salt, pepper, paprika, cumin, coriander, garlic powder, and onion. Thread ground meat mixture carefully around 8 skewers. Place in refrigerator at least 4 hours to develop flavors.

Heat argan oil in a medium sauté pan over medium-high heat. Add onion and sauté until translucent, approximately 5 minutes. Add garlic and sauté for 1 minute or until fragrant. Add tomatos, cumin, paprika, coriander, salt, pepper, harissa, and honey. Bring to a boil and reduce to a simmer. Continue simmering uncovered until all the liquid has evaporated, approximately 30 minutes. Adjust seasoning to taste.

Heat grill that has been greased with olive oil. Grill köfte until medium, approximately 2-3 minutes per side. Serve over tomato coulis with Moroccan green olives and fresh arugula to garnish.

Roasted Pepper and Tomato Salad

One of the most traditional of all the salads in North Africa. Roasting the peppers brings out their natural sugars, making them sweeter and easier to digest. I haven't met a single person who claims not to like peppers whom I haven't converted with this one. Like I always say, it isn't the ingredient you don't like, it is the preparation of it.

YIELDS 8 SERVINGS

6 red, yellow, or orange
   bell peppers
2 28-oz cans whole peeled
   tomatoes
2 Tbsp argan or extra
   virgin olive oil
1 Tbsp red wine vinegar
2-3 garlic cloves, minced
1 Tbsp harissa

Pinch kosher salt and
   freshly ground pepper
1-2 tsp Hungarian hot
   paprika
1-2 tsp ground cumin
2 Tbsp Italian parsley,
   finely chopped
2 Tbsp cilantro, finely
   chopped

Place peppers directly over open flame of a gas burner, rotating periodically. Char until skins are completely black. Place in a Ziploc bag and seal. (If you do not have a gas stove, place peppers on a baking sheet in a 375 degree oven for approximately 25 minutes, rotating periodically, until the skins begin to blacken. Place in Ziploc and continue recipe as written.) Allow to sit for at least 10 minutes so the skins peel off easily. Remove blackened skins and seeds. Dice roasted peppers. Empty cans of tomato into a large mixing bowl. Using your hands, crush the tomatoes completely. Cook tomatoes in a large sauté pan over medium-high heat for approximately 30 minutes or until all the liquid has reduced. Add argan or olive oil, vinegar, and garlic. Sauté for a minute or until garlic is fragrant. Add peppers. Season with salt, pepper, paprika, cumin, parsley, cilantro, and harissa. Continue cooking until all the liquid has evaporated. Season to taste. Cool completely and refrigerate. Allow to sit in the refrigerator for at least 2 hours or overnight to develop the flavors. Serve at room temperature.

Majoun

Majoun translates as "love potion" in Arabic. It originally included kif, which is the Moroccan equivalent of cannabis and was considered a delicacy. This version uses the basic recipe that has been adapted for use by Moroccan Jews who came to the area in droves during the Spanish Inquisition. It was a natural adaptation for use during the Passover Seder as the haroseth, or fruit and nut mixture which was eaten as a representation of the mortar the Jews used to build the Pyramids during their enslavement by the Egyptians.

YIELDS APPROXIMATELY 12 SERVINGS

1 cup pitted dates
½ cup raisins
¼ cup walnuts
¼ cup slivered almonds
1 tsp freshly grated nutmeg
½ tsp ground cloves
1 tsp ground ginger

1 tsp ground cinnamon
2-3 Tbsp orange flower water
½-1 cup Manischewitz kosher grape or blackberry flavored wine
Sesame seeds for garnish

Place all the ingredients in a food processor. Process to combine, adding wine as needed until the mixture forms a smooth paste. Remove from processor and place in the refrigerator for approximately 30 minutes to harden. Roll into approximately ½" confections and garnish with sesame seeds. Keep in the refrigerator in an airtight container for up to 3 weeks.

Moroccan Dinner

I consider Moroccan food and culture to be my ultimate specialty. Having written on Moroccan Tea Ritual for my master's thesis, which was published in early 2010, and having spent time in Morocco taking cooking classes from locals, I feel a particular kinship to the culture. Moroccan food is complex and yet very basic in terms of its use of spices and fresh, seasonal fruits and vegetables. A largely Muslim culture, Morocco is geographically situated in a place where it has been occupied by everyone seeking the strategic advantage of its location. As such, the food is representative of many different cultures from Spanish and French, a product of the colonial period, to Middle Eastern and Jewish, a product of the Spanish Inquisition when many Jews fled Spain to Morocco.

A couple of unique facts about Morocco's relationship to the United States: Morocco was the first county to recognize the U.S. as a sovereign nation, in 1777, and we have the longest standing trade agreements with Morocco. Finally, like other Middle Eastern and Mediterranean cuisines, Moroccan cuisine is ideally suited to a gluten-free lifestyle. Besides bread, most of the foods of Morocco are composed primarily of meats, vegetables, and spices and therefore gluten-free.

Moroccan Quick Bread

Bread is a staple of the Moroccan diet. It is used as a utensil, as most people eat with their hands, to sop up the sauces and dressings from the delicious salads and stews that are served at a typical Moroccan meal. This bread is simple, gluten-free, and allows for that sopping up of wonderful flavors.

YIELDS 8 SERVINGS

1 Tbsp unsalted butter, softened

2 cups Domata Living Flour

1 tsp kosher salt

2 tsp baking powder

½ tsp baking soda

2 Tbsp sugar

1 tsp ground cinnamon

1 stick unsalted butter, cubed

1 cup buttermilk (see p. 162)

1 egg

1 tsp pure vanilla extract

1 Tbsp orange blossom water

Preheat oven to 375 degrees.

Grease a loaf pan with butter. Combine flour, salt, baking powder, baking soda, sugar, and cinnamon in a medium mixing bowl. Using a pastry cutter, incorporate butter until the mixture resembles small peas. Combine buttermilk with egg, vanilla, and orange blossom water and add to dry mix. Using a fork, stir until just combined. Pour batter into loaf pan and bake for approximately 35 to 40 minutes or until the bread is golden and a toothpick inserted into the center of the loaf comes out clean. Cool completely before serving.

Eggplant Chips

Jeff and I first had these at the Djemma El Fna food fair in Marrakech. They served them at many of the stalls as a side dish, not unlike you would see French fries served here in the U.S. Needless to say, we ate about a pound of them each. They are that good.

YIELDS APPROXIMATELY 6-8 SERVINGS

*1 large globe eggplant or
  3-4 Japanese eggplant,
  sliced ¼" thick
Kosher salt*

*Freshly ground pepper
2-3 garlic cloves, minced
Olive oil for frying*

Lay slices of eggplant on paper towels and sprinkle liberally with salt. Cover with another layer of paper towels and allow to sit for about an hour. Heat olive oil in a large sauté pan. Fry eggplant slices until crisp and golden, approximately 5 minutes per side. Season with freshly ground pepper and sprinkle with fresh garlic. Serve immediately.

Moroccan Relish

This basic mixed vegetable salad is typical throughout the Middle East and North Africa. My fondest memory of it is from the middle of the Sahara desert. We were on a camel trek when we stopped for lunch. Abdul, our tour guide, pulled out all the vegetables, chopped them up, and seasoned them. He opened a can of Moroccan sardines, and lunch was served. It is one of the best things I have ever eaten in my life. This is likely a product of three things: one, fresh vegetables; two, incredible Moroccan sardines; and three, ambiance.

YIELDS APPROXIMATELY 8 SERVINGS

½ red onion, diced
1 pint grape tomatoes, halved
1 English cucumber, peeled, seeded and diced
1 green bell pepper, seeded and diced
2-3 garlic cloves, minced

Kosher salt and freshly ground pepper
2 tsp ground cumin
2 tsp Hungarian smoked hot paprika
3-4 Tbsp extra virgin olive oil
2-3 Tbsp red wine vinegar

Combine veggies in a mixing bowl. Drizzle with oil and vinegar. Season to taste with salt, pepper, cumin, and paprika. Allow to marinate at least one hour or overnight before serving. Serve at room temperature.

Roasted Beet Salad

Beets are amazingly high in sugar. Roasting them brings out these natural sugars and gives them a nutty flavor that is delicious paired with the sweet spices in this salad. If you can get them, beets come in multiple colors besides just the deep purple of regular beets. You can get golden, multi-colored, and even one that is like a candy cane. Use an assortment for a really beautiful presentation.

YIELDS APPROXIMATELY 8 SERVINGS

1 lb medium beets
2-3 Tbsp extra virgin olive oil
Kosher salt and freshly ground pepper
2-3 Tbsp argan oil
2 Tbsp orange blossom water

1 tsp ground cinnamon
½ tsp ground ginger
½ tsp anise seed
Kosher salt and freshly ground pepper
4 oz goat cheese
2-3 garlic cloves, minced
½ red onion, sliced

Cut off ends of beets. Place beets on a baking sheet. Drizzle with olive oil and season with salt and pepper. Place in a 375 degree oven for 45 minutes to 1 hour or until tender. Let cool. Peel and slice the beets. Place on a serving dish. Season with salt, pepper, cinnamon, ginger, anise seed, garlic, and onion. Drizzle with argan oil and orange water. Garnish with cheese.

Orange and Olive Salad

A traditional Moroccan salad, this one always catches people by surprise. Many can't imagine a salad with both oranges and garlic in it. The key ingredients are the argan oil and the orange blossom water. I discuss the argan in the introduction to this book so I won't go into detail here, but the orange blossom water is a specialty ingredient that is worth mentioning. It is made through a steam distillation process, not unlike perfume. Orange blossoms are boiled in water, the steam is captured in a siphon, and then re-condensed into a liquid. The result is something completely unique that at times smells more like you should wear it than eat it.

6 oranges, peeled and cut
   into segments
3-4 garlic cloves, minced
½ cup of pitted Moroccan
   black or kalamata
   olives
1 tsp ground cumin

½-1 tsp Hungarian hot
   paprika
Pinch kosher salt and
   freshly ground pepper
1 Tbsp orange blossom
   water
2 Tbsp argan oil

Arrange orange segments on a platter. Garnish with garlic and olives. Season with cumin, paprika, salt and pepper. Drizzle with orange water and argan oil. Serve at room temperature.

Feta, Tomato, and Preserved Lemon Salad

As you have already noticed, when Moroccans call something a salad, they don't simply mean lettuce, tomatoes, and cucumbers. Salads are made with virtually any fresh vegetable. Here is yet another classic salad utilizing preserved lemons.

YIELDS APPROXIMATELY **8** SERVINGS

4 oz feta cheese
3 tomatoes, sliced
1 preserved lemon (see p.
   43), peel only, rinsed
   and chopped
½ red onion, sliced
2-3 garlic cloves, minced

2-3 Tbsp extra virgin
   olive oil
2 Tbsp red wine vinegar
Pinch kosher salt and
   freshly ground pepper
1 tsp ground cumin
1 tsp Hungarian hot
   paprika

Layer tomatoes on a plate. Garnish with lemon, onion, garlic, and feta. Drizzle with olive oil and vinegar and season with salt, pepper, cumin, and paprika. Serve at room temperature.

Chicken and Butternut Squash Tagine

The term "tagine" refers not only to a stew but to the specific conical shaped clay pots these stews are cooked in. They can be made from an almost endless combination of vegetables, meats, and spices. Moroccans are only limited by what they can find fresh at the market on a daily basis.

YIELDS APPROXIMATELY 8 SERVINGS

2 lbs boneless, skinless chicken thighs
1 onion, diced
2-3 garlic cloves, minced
¼ cup Italian parsley, chopped
¼ cup cilantro, chopped
Pinch kosher salt and freshly ground pepper
2 tsp ground cinnamon
1 tsp ground coriander
1 tsp ground ginger

Pinch saffron
2 cups chicken broth
1 butternut squash, peeled, seeded, and cut into 1" cubes
½ cup toasted whole blanched almonds
1 can chickpeas, drained
1 Tbsp honey
2 Tbsp extra virgin olive oil
2 Tbsp unsalted butter

Heat olive oil and butter in a medium sauté pan over medium-high heat. Add chicken and brown on both sides, approximately 3 minutes per side. Add onion and sauté until just translucent, approximately 5 minutes. Add garlic and sauté for 1 minute until fragrant. Season with salt, pepper, cinnamon, coriander, ginger, and saffron. Sauté for 1 minute to toast spices. Add chicken broth and bring to a boil. Cover and reduce to a simmer. Continue cooking for approximately 45 minutes. Add squash and more broth if needed. Cover and bring to a boil. Reduce heat to a simmer and continue cooking until the squash is tender, approximately 20 minutes. Add parsley, cilantro, chickpeas, and honey. Season to taste. Serve hot, garnished with toasted almonds.

Moroccan Fruit Salad

Morocco is not typically known for elaborate desserts. While French style cafes have popped up in the more modern quarters of the major cities where you can find French style pastries, you don't generally see them served at the end of a meal. Most meals are topped off with fresh or dried fruit, nuts, and of course a pot of mint tea.

YIELDS APPROXIMATELY 8 SERVINGS

3 cups assorted fresh
   fruit, cubed
1 tsp ground cinnamon

1 Tbsp orange blossom
   water
2-3 Tbsp honey

Arrange fruit neatly on a platter. Garnish with cinnamon, orange blossom water, and honey.

Greek Dinner

Hopa! Who hasn't seen the movie "My Big Fat Greek Wedding"? Greek families and Greece in general are known for fantastic food. Often times, however, people think of items like spanikopita or bakhlava, which are pastry-based items and obviously not suitable for a gluten-free lifestyle. However, those are just the tip of the iceberg. There are many Greek recipes that lend themselves to a gluten-free menu with little or no adjustments. Here are a few of my favorites.

Greek-Style Chilled Cucumber Soup

When you think of soup, most people think of hot soups. Cold soups can be a delightful and refreshing addition to a summer menu, taking advantage of all the fresh vegetables and herbs of the season. This one also happens to be incredibly easy and can be made in advance for a party so you don't have to babysit it to keep it warm.

YIELDS APPROXIMATELY 8 SERVINGS

3 English cucumbers, peeled, seeded, and chopped
1 Spanish or Vidalia onion, diced
4 garlic cloves, minced
1 avocado, chopped
Kosher salt and freshly ground pepper
¼ cup mint, chopped
¼ cup chives, snipped

2 tsp dried dillweed
½ cup feta, crumbled
1 Tbsp harissa
16 oz plain Greek yogurt (Fage is a good brand)
½-¾ cup Daisy sour cream
¾ cup lemon juice
½ cup heavy cream
¼ cup extra virgin olive oil

Combine all the ingredients in a large bowl. Blend using an immersion blender until creamy and well combined. Adjust seasoning to taste. Serve with crumbled feta and cilantro oil.

Dolmades (Stuffed Grape Leaves)

These can be made hot or cold, with meat or meatless. As a first course I prefer the meatless version, which is the recipe I give you here. These will keep for about a week in the fridge, so make extra for leftovers. I actually love them for breakfast.

For the filling
- 2 Tbsp extra virgin olive oil
- 2 Tbsp unsalted butter
- 3-4 shallots, minced
- 4 scallions, chopped
- 3-4 garlic cloves, minced
- 1 cup basmati rice, rinsed and soaked for 30 minutes, then drained
- Kosher salt and freshly ground pepper
- 2 tsp dried oregano
- 2 tsp dried dillweed
- 2½ cups Kitchen Basics, Pacifica, or Progresso chicken broth
- ½ cup chopped Italian parsley
- ½ cup chopped peppermint
- ½ cup chopped cilantro
- ¼ cup toasted pine nuts
- ¼ cup dried currants or dried cranberries
- 4 large tomatoes, diced

For the layers
- 2-3 Tbsp extra virgin olive oil
- ¼-½ cup lemon juice
- 2 large tomatoes, sliced
- 20-25 brined grape leaves (These can come in a jar or in a vacuum- sealed package. Either way, they should be soaked in hot water for 10 minutes and rinsed before using to remove the saline brine.)

Heat oil and butter in a medium sauté pan over medium-high heat until the butter has melted and is bubbling. Add shallots and scallions. Sauté for a minute or two or until they begin to turn golden. Add the garlic and sauté for 1 minute or until fragrant. Add rice, salt, pepper, oregano, and dillweed, and sauté for 1 minute to toast the rice. Add 2 cups chicken broth and bring to a boil. Cover and reduce heat to a simmer. Cook for approximately 16 minutes or until all the liquid has been absorbed. Don't peek. Rice won't cook if you remove the lid. Fluff rice with a fork and transfer to a bowl to allow to cool. Once it has cooled, add parsley, mint, cilantro, chopped tomatoes, pine nuts, and dried currants or cranberries. Toss well to combine and adjust seasoning to taste.

Prepare large stockpot for cooking. Drizzle bottom with olive oil and layer with sliced tomatoes. To assemble dolmades, take each grape leaf and trim the stem. Place approximately 1 Tbsp of filling at base of the leaf. Fold over the edges and roll the leaf up like a burrito. Place on bottom of stockpot. Continue until the bottom of pan is covered with a single layer of dolmades. Drizzle with more olive oil and some lemon juice. Continue assembling and layering dolmades until all the filling is used up, drizzling with lemon juice and olive oil between each layer. Cover approximately ½ full with chicken broth. Use a smaller plate on top of the dolmades to weigh them down so that they don't unravel during the cooking process.

Bring to a boil over medium-high heat. Cover and reduce to a simmer. Cook for approximately 20-30 minutes or until the broth begins to bubble around the edges of the plate. Remove from heat and allow to cool completely in the pan. Either serve at room temperature or refrigerate and serve cold. They can be made a couple of days in advance and kept in the refrigerator.

Pastitsio

Literally translated this is "macaroni pie," which at face value would seem to be a problem as noodles are not gluten-free. However, there are corn and rice noodles nowadays that taste and work very much like wheat pastas. You can use them interchangeably in almost any pasta dish and the whole family will love it, regardless of whether they have gluten intolerance or not.

YIELDS APPROXIMATELY 8 SERVINGS

1 lb ground lamb or
  ground beef
2 large onions, diced
3-4 garlic cloves, minced
2 Tbsp extra virgin olive
  oil
3-4 Tbsp tomato paste
¼-½ cup dry sherry or
  dry vermouth
¼ cup chopped Italian
  parsley
Kosher salt and freshly
  ground pepper
2 tsp ground cinnamon
2 tsp dried oregano
1 tsp ground coriander
1 tsp ground allspice
Pinch freshly grated
  nutmeg
1 lb corn macaroni,
  cooked according to
package directions al
dente (my personal
favorite is Orgran,
but sometimes it is
hard to find, so any
gluten-free brand
will work)
1 cup shredded Gruyère
  or Asiago

For the sauce
½ cup unsalted butter
½ cup Domata Living
  Flour
Kosher salt and freshly
  ground pepper
Pinch freshly grated
  nutmeg
2 cups whole milk

Heat olive oil in a medium sauté pan over medium-high heat. Add onions and sauté until translucent, approximately 5 minutes. Add garlic and sauté for 1 minute or until fragrant. Add ground meat and season with salt, pepper, cinnamon, oregano, coriander, allspice, and nutmeg. Continue cooking until the meat is browned. Add tomato paste and stir through. Add parsley and sherry or vermouth. Continue cooking uncovered until the sauce has thickened. Adjust seasoning to taste. Toss with macaroni to combine.

Melt butter in a small saucepan over medium heat. Add Domata flour and whisk to combine. Cook for approximately 1 minute to cook rawness out of flour. Add milk and season with salt, pepper, and nutmeg. Continue to whisk until the sauce has thickened. Adjust seasoning to taste.

Grease a 9" x 11" Pyrex baking dish with butter. Place macaroni/ meat mixture in bottom of the dish. Top with sauce and finally shredded cheese. Bake in a preheated 375 degree oven for approximately 20 minutes or until the top is bubbling and golden brown. Allow to sit at room temperature for approximately 10 minutes before serving.

Rizopita

This literally translates to "rice pie." This dessert is a lot like a rice pudding, although perhaps a thicker, more cake-like version of it. I tend to prefer it to rice pudding because it is easier to serve and it reheats beautifully.

Yields Approximately 12 Servings

½ lb basmati rice, cooked
4 eggs
½ cup sugar
¾ cup Carnation evaporated milk
1 lb fresh whole milk ricotta
1 tsp ground cinnamon
Pinch ground cloves
Pinch freshly grated nutmeg
1 tsp pure vanilla extract
1 Tbsp orange blossom water
1 tsp lemon zest
½ cup melted unsalted butter

Preheat oven to 350 degrees.

Beat eggs and sugar. Add evaporated milk and beat till smooth. Add ricotta and stir to combine. Add cinnamon, lemon zest, cloves, vanilla, orange water, and nutmeg. Stir to combine. Add rice and butter and stir to combine. Place in a 12" round baking pan that has been greased with Pam cooking spray. Bake for 1 hour or until golden brown. Serve hot.

Italian Dinner

When most of us think of Italian food, pizza and pasta come to mind. Lately a number of gluten-free options have popped up in both of these categories. Gluten-free pizza crusts are now commercially available, and many pizza places are offering gluten-free crust options. I personally find the commercially available pizza crusts to be gummy so I prefer to stay away from them. As previously mentioned, the pasta options are great. Very much like wheat pastas and readily available.

Three Bean and Spinach Soup

I happen to love puréed soups, and this one is no exception. It has the added bonus of being really healthy with the protein and fiber of beans and the iron from the spinach, so eat up!

YIELDS APPROXIMATELY 8 SERVINGS

1 onion, finely chopped
3-4 garlic cloves, minced
1 carrot, peeled and diced
2 celery stalks, diced
3 Tbsp extra virgin olive oil
½ cup dry vermouth or sherry
8 cups chicken broth (I prefer Kitchen Basics, Pacifia or Progresso.)
1 can cannelini or great northern beans, drained

1 can light red kidney beans, drained
1 can chickpeas, drained
1 tsp kosher salt
½ tsp pepper
1 tsp Hungarian smoked hot paprika
1 Tbsp herbes de Provence
2 bay leaves
1 lb baby spinach leaves
2 Tbsp Pecorino Romano or Parmigiano Reggiano cheese, freshly grated

Place stockpot over medium-high heat. Add onions and sauté for approximately 8 minutes or until tender and just slightly golden. Add garlic and cook 1 minute or until fragrant. Add carrots and celery and cook for 5 minutes or until the vegetables begin to soften. Add seasonings and deglaze pan with vermouth or sherry. Continue cooking until most of the liquid has evaporated. Add beans and chicken broth. Bring to a boil. Cover and reduce heat to a simmer. Cook for approximately 45 minutes. Remove bay leaves and purée soup with an immersion blender. Pass puréed soup through a fine mesh sieve. Return strained soup to stockpot and adjust seasonings to taste. Add spinach and return to a boil. Cover and reduce to a simmer. Continue cooking another 15 minutes or until most of the spinach has wilted. Add freshly grated cheese as garnish and serve hot with crusty bread.

Mozzarella Caprese Salad

A classic Italian salad. No matter how often I have eaten it and how simple it is to make, I always order this at an Italian restaurant. This salad is ideal for summer when you have an abundance of fresh ripe tomatoes of all kinds. Mix up the colors of the tomatoes for an exceptionally beautiful presentation.

YIELDS 4 SERVINGS

4 tsp good quality balsamic vinegar or balsamic reduction (see p. 38)

4 Tbsp extra virgin olive oil

12 cherry tomatoes, halved or 24 grape tomatoes

4 Roma, green zebra, yellow or orange tomatoes, quartered

8 fresh basil leaves

8 oz. fresh mozzarella (You can find this in specialty stores and in the deli section of some grocery stores. It is packed in water and comes in either one larger boule or a package of little ones called bocconcini, which is what I prefer for this salad)

To assemble the salad, divide the tomatoes and mozzarella evenly amongst 4 plates. Season with salt and pepper. Top with 1 Tbsp olive oil and 1 tsp balsamic vinegar. Garnish with a pinch of freshly chopped basil leaves. Serve immediately.

Gluten-Free Chicken Parmesan with Homemade Pasta Sauce and Corn Pasta

OK, this one blows almost everyone away. Chicken Parmesan definitely seems like something you couldn't possibly have on a gluten-free diet. Yet it is really quite simple to make. The key is homemade marinara sauce. You can't and shouldn't buy store bought sauces. (A) You can't guarantee they don't have items in them that aren't potentially dangerous on a gluten-free diet, and (B) There are a ton of preservatives in them, which as far as I'm concerned is bad for any diet, gluten-free or otherwise.

YIELDS 4 SERVINGS

For the sauce
- 2 Tbsp extra virgin olive oil
- 2 Tbsp unsalted butter
- 1 onion, diced
- 2-3 garlic cloves, minced
- 1 carrot, peeled and diced
- 1 celery stalk, diced
- 2 28-oz cans whole peeled tomatoes, crushed by hand
- ¼-½ cup dry vermouth or dry sherry
- Kosher salt and freshly ground pepper
- 2 tsp harissa or pinch of crushed red pepper
- 1 bay leaf
- 2 tsp Italian seasoning
- Handful fresh Italian parsley, chopped
- Handful basil, torn
- 2 Tbsp honey

For the chicken
- 4 boneless skinless chicken breasts
- ½ cup Domata Living Flour
- 2 eggs
- 1 Tbsp whole milk
- ½ cup almond meal
- ¼ cup grated Parmesan cheese
- 1 tsp Italian seasoning
- Kosher salt and freshly ground pepper
- Pam cooking spray
- Olive oil to pan fry chicken breasts
- 4 slices provolone (I prefer having the deli slice it fresh rather than buying prepackaged sliced cheese.)
- 1 lb corn or rice pasta

Heat 2 Tbsp oil and 2 Tbsp butter in a medium sauce pan over medium-high heat. Add onion and sauté until translucent, approximately 5 minutes. Add garlic and sauté 1 minute or until fragrant. Add carrot, celery, salt, pepper, bay leaf, crushed red pepper, and Italian seasoning. Sauté a couple of minutes to toast spices and soften vegetables. Add vermouth and cook until most of the liquid has evaporated. Add tomatoes and bring to a boil. Reduce heat to a simmer and simmer uncovered, approximately 45 minutes or until most of the liquid has evaporated and the sauce has thickened. Remove bay leaf and add parsley and basil. Add honey and purée sauce with an immersion blender to desired texture. Adjust seasoning to taste.

For the chicken, place each chicken breast between two pieces of plastic wrap and pound to approximately ½" thick with a meat mallet. Season Domata flour with salt and pepper. Combine eggs and milk and season with salt and pepper. Combine almond meal, Parmesan, and Italian seasoning, and season with salt and pepper. Dredge each chicken breast first in flour mixture, then in egg batter, then in almond meal mixture. Transfer to a baking sheet.

Heat approximately ½" of olive oil in a large sauté pan over medium-high heat. Pan fry chicken breasts until golden brown on each side, approximately 3-4 minutes per side. Transfer to a baking dish that has been greased with Pam cooking spray. Top each chicken breast with approximately ¼ cup of sauce or enough to coat entire breast. Top again with one slice of provolone per breast. Preheat oven to 375 degrees. Bake chicken breasts for approximately 20-30 minutes or until the cheese has melted and begins to brown. Serve hot over freshly cooked corn or rice pasta.

Zabaglione with Fresh Fruit

Call it custard, call it meringue, call it whatever you'd like. I call it delicious, light, and unique. This variation is a Moroccan play on the Italian classic.

YIELDS APPROXIMATELY 4-6 SERVINGS

4 egg yolks
4 tsp sugar
4 Tbsp Pinot Grigio
1 Tbsp orange blossom
  water

1 tsp pure vanilla extract
1 tsp ground cinnamon
Fresh fruit to garnish

Place all the ingredients in a heatproof bowl. Bring a small saucepan of water to a boil. Place bowl over saucepan and reduce heat to a simmer. Whisk vigorously until the mixture thickens to the consistency of yogurt. Remove from heat and cool. Cover and place in the refrigerator for approximately 3 hours to cool. Spoon into small serving bowls and garnish with fresh fruit.

Italian food is so popular and so diverse it seemed appropriate to include another complete menu in this book. Again, feel free to mix and match.

Prosciutto-Wrapped Artichoke Hearts with Pesto and Balsamic Reduction

Prosciutto is a cured Italian ham. It is salty and delicious, so it pairs really well with the mild fresh mozzarella. If you can, try to purchase the prosciutto in a package where the slices are separated with butcher paper or have it sliced fresh. The fatty ham tends to stick, making it impossible to pull slices apart without ripping them.

YIELDS APPROXIMATELY 12 SERVINGS

1 batch homemade pesto
(see recipe under
Monika's Mousse)
12 slices prosciutto
12 balls fresh mozzarella
(bocconcini, which are
the smaller ones, or you
can slice a larger ball
of fresh mozzarella and
cut it into 24 pieces)
2 cans artichoke quarters
(not marinated)
Balsamic reduction to
garnish (see p. 38)

Preheat oven to 350 degrees.

Slice each piece of prosciutto in half vertically and each bocconcini in half. Wrap a half portion of prosciutto around a piece of mozzarella and a quarter piece of artichoke heart. Place on baking sheet. Continue wrapping all of the artichoke heart pieces and mozzarella until none remain. Bake for approximately 10 minutes or until the mozzarella begins to melt.

To serve, place a dollop of pesto over each wrap and drizzle with balsamic reduction.

Grilled Vegetable Napoleon
with Roasted Garlic Aioli, Sopressata Crisp, Parmesan Tuile, and Balsamic Reduction

While a napoleon is historically a pastry filled with custard, I developed this recipe as a play on words. The grilled vegetables act as the pastry layers and the aioli as the custard. It is a wonderful salad course that you can use as an alternative to a caprese salad in the fall or winter when tomatoes aren't exactly ripe. It also has spectacular stage presence. Just a lovely presentation that always impresses guests.

YIELDS 4 SERVINGS

4 slices Boar's Head
   sopressata
1 cup freshly grated
   Parmesan cheese
1 head garlic
1 Tbsp extra virgin olive
   oil
½ cup Hellmanns
   mayonnaise
2 Tbsp whole milk
Pinch kosher salt and
   freshly ground pepper

4 portabella mushrooms
1 large red bell pepper,
   seeds removed, cut into
   4 slices
1 small red onion, cut into
   4 slices, ¼" thick
1 small eggplant, cut into
   4 slices, ½" thick
Pam cooking spray
½ cup balsamic reduction
   (see page 38)

For the sopressata crisps
Place on a baking sheet and bake in a 350 degree oven about 10 minutes or until the salami has crisped up like bacon. Cool.

For the Parmesan tuiles
Divide grated Parmesan into 4 equal piles on a baking sheet lined with parchment paper. Place in a 350 degree oven for approximately 10-15 minutes or until the Parmesan has melted and become crispy. Cool.

For the roasted garlic aioli
Remove any of the outside paper of the garlic as possible. Place on a sheet of aluminum foil and drizzle liberally with olive oil. Seal foil tightly and place on a baking sheet. Bake in a 350 degree oven for approximately 1 hour. Cool. Squeeze all the roasted garlic out of the head into a bowl and combine with the mayonnaise, milk, and a pinch of salt and pepper. Chill.

For the veggies
Season an indoor grill pan with cooking spray. Heat on medium-high heat. Grill veggies on both sides to create nice grill marks and season liberally with salt and pepper.

To assemble napoleon
Place eggplant on the bottom, red onion next, portabella mushroom next, and top with the grilled bell peppers. Top each napoleon with about a tablespoon of the garlic aioli. Drizzle the balsamic reduction around the napoleon and garnish with one sopressata crisp and one Parmesan tuile. Serve immediately.

Minestrone

I have had numerous people refer to this soup affectionately as "leftover" or "garbage" soup because historically it is made with leftover vegetables. However, I think it is a delicious vegetable soup in its own right. I prefer to think of it as a soup that takes advantage of whatever vegetable happens to be in season. Use this recipe as a base, but keep in mind seasonality. This is obviously a summer variation with summer vegetables. In the winter you may substitute with more root vegetables.

YIELDS APPROXIMATELY 8-10 SERVINGS

4 oz Canadian bacon, diced

1 large onion, chopped

2-3 garlic cloves, minced

2-3 Tbsp extra virgin olive oil

1 carrot, peeled and chopped

2 celery stalks, chopped

2 russet or Kennebec potatoes, peeled and chopped

1 zucchini, diced

1 yellow squash, diced

1 can dark red kidney beans, drained

½ cup basil leaves, torn

½ cup Italian parsley, chopped

Kosher salt and freshly ground pepper

Pinch red pepper flakes

2 Tbsp Italian seasoning

2 bay leaves

½ cup dry vermouth or dry sherry

1 28-oz can whole peeled tomatoes, crushed

8 cups Kitchen Basics, Pacifica, or Progresso chicken broth

½ cup freshly grated Parmigiano Reggiano cheese

Heat olive oil in a large stockpot over medium-high heat. Add Canadian bacon and sauté until the bacon begins to caramelize. Add the onion and continue cooking approximately 5 minutes or until the onion begins to soften and turn translucent. Add garlic and cook 1 minute or until fragrant. Add carrots, celery, and potato and sauté for approximately 8 minutes or until they begin to soften. Add salt, pepper, red pepper flakes, Italian seasoning, and bay leaves. Deglaze the pan with the vermouth or sherry and continue cooking, uncovered, until the liquid has evaporated. Add tomatoes and chicken broth and bring to a boil. Cover and reduce to a simmer. Cook for approximately 45 minutes. Remove cover and add the zucchini, squash, basil, parsley, and kidney beans. Bring back to a boil and cover. Reduce heat to a simmer and cook an additional 15 minutes. Season to taste. Serve hot with freshly grated Parmigiano Reggiano on top.

Chicken Cacciatore

This dish is known as "Hunter's Stew." It is a rustic one-pot meal that makes for delicious leftovers. It reheats well and again benefits from marinating.

2 Tbsp extra virgin olive oil
2 Tbsp unsalted butter
3-4 garlic cloves, minced
1 large onion, diced
Kosher salt and freshly ground pepper
1 tsp harissa or pinch of crushed red pepper flakes
1 Tbsp herbes de Provence or Italian seasoning
2 lbs boneless, skinless chicken thighs

½ cup red wine vinegar
3 14-oz cans fire-roasted tomatoes
Handful fresh basil, torn
½ cup dry sherry or dry vermouth
1 cup pitted kalamata olives
2 red peppers, seeded and sliced
1 lb button or cremini mushrooms, stems removed, peeled and sliced

Heat oil and butter in a large skillet over medium-high heat until melted. Add onion and sauté for 1 minute or until fragrant. Add chicken, salt, pepper, harissa or pepper flakes, and herbes de Provence and sauté until chicken is lightly browned, approximately 10 minutes. Add vinegar and simmer until reduced by half. Add tomatoes and bring to a boil. Reduce to a simmer and cook uncovered for approximately 30 minutes or until the liquid has reduced completely. Add basil, vermouth or sherry, olives, pepper, and mushrooms and bring to a boil. Reduce heat to a simmer and allow to cook uncovered until the sauce has thickened and the peppers are cooked through, approximately an additional 15 minutes. Adjust seasoning to taste.

Herb-Roasted Acorn Squash

One of my favorite side dishes, this is easy and filling. You can also use this as a base for an acorn squash soup, using the same basic recipe as the roasted butternut squash soup. Simply cool and scoop the roasted squash out of the peel. Then use it the same way you use the butternut squash in the recipe.

YIELDS 4 SERVINGS

1 acorn squash
2 Tbsp extra virgin olive oil
Kosher salt and freshly ground pepper
1 Tbsp Hungarian hot paprika
1 Tbsp garlic powder

1 Tbsp herbes de Provence or Italian seasoning
Pinch freshly grated nutmeg
1 Tbsp freshly grated Parmesan cheese
1 Tbsp honey

Preheat oven to 375 degrees.

Cut off both ends of acorn squash. Quarter squash. Scoop out seeds. Place quarters on a baking sheet. Drizzle with olive oil. Season each quarter evenly with salt, pepper, paprika, garlic powder, herbes de Provence, nutmeg, Parmesan, and honey. Bake for approximately 45 minutes or until the squash is just cooked through and begins to caramelize.

Ricotta Cheesecake with Raspberry Sauce

I have never been a huge cheesecake kind of gal, but this cheesecake I will eat an entire serving of. It is much lighter and fluffier and far less sweet, so you can enjoy it after a substantial meal without feeling weighed down. Incidentally, cheesecake was invented in Italy and originally made with ricotta, so you'll feel like you're enjoying a little piece of history, too.

YIELDS APPROXIMATELY 10 SERVINGS

6 eggs, separated
⅔ cup granulated sugar
1 lb whole milk ricotta
2 Tbsp Domata Living Flour
2 Tbsp mascarpone cream (not the kind that already has chocolate and coffee in it for tiramisu) or Daisy sour cream

1 Tbsp orange zest
1 Tbsp orange blossom water
1 tsp pure vanilla extract
¼ tsp ground cinnamon
Pinch kosher salt
Pinch cream of tartar
Pam cooking spray
½ cup seedless raspberry jam
1 Tbsp water

Preheat oven to 350 degrees. Place egg yolks and sugar in a food processor and blend until pale yellow and combined, approximately 30 seconds. Add ricotta, flour, mascarpone, orange zest, orange blossom water, cinnamon, and vanilla, and continue to blend until well combined. In a separate bowl, beat egg whites with cream of tartar and a pinch of salt until stiff peaks form. Pour egg yolk mixture down the side of the bowl of whipped egg whites and fold gently to combine. Pour cheesecake batter into a greased 10" springform pan. Place pan in a baking dish to catch any drips and place in the oven. Bake for approximately 45 minutes or until golden brown and just set. Remove from oven and immediately run a paring knife around the edge of the cake to remove it from the side of the pan. Cool completely and refrigerate before serving. For the sauce, place preserves and water in a small saucepan. Bring to a boil and simmer until the sauce is syrupy and thickened. Serve immediately.

Mexican Fiesta

O le! I love a Cinco de Mayo party. And to top this one off, make some Margaritas. Tequila is made from the agave plant and is not a grain-distilled alcohol, so in general it is safe to drink. I recommend Jose Cuervo, which is guaranteed gluten-free. Do not use commercially produced Margarita mix. Try mixing two parts tequila to one part lime juice and one part orange juice. Sweeten with some agave nectar, which is a natural sweetener available at most grocery stores. Place in a martini shaker with ice and serve in a martini glass that has been salted around the rim.

Guacamole

To me no Mexican meal is complete without guacamole. Obviously the key to this one is to find absolutely ripe avocadoes. What you want to look for are fruits (yes, avocadoes are a fruit) that are black, have a give to them when you press them, and aren't moldy or mushy at the top where the stem was attached. Avocadoes should never be refrigerated until after they have been used. They should be kept in a cool dry place alongside your apples, onions, and other vegetables and fruits. To ripen an unripe avocado, place it in a window sill that gets plenty of direct sunlight. The avocado will ripen within 24 hours. To store a partially used avocado, leave the seed in the half you plan to store, which will keep it from browning, place in a Ziploc baggie and put in the refrigerator.

YIELDS APPROXIMATELY 8 SERVINGS
(OR IF I'M INVITED TO THE PARTY, MAYBE 4)

4 ripe avocadoes
1-2 jalapeños, roasted (see p. 87), peeled and minced
½ red onion, minced
2-3 garlic cloves, minced
1 Roma tomato, seeded and finely chopped

Pinch kosher salt and freshly ground pepper
1 lemon
1 tsp ground cumin
1 tsp Hungarian hot paprika
2 Tbsp cilantro, chopped
1 Tbsp harissa

For a spicier guacamole, leave the seeds and the vein of the jalapeño in the pepper. For a milder guacamole, remove the seeds and veins before mincing. Add chopped tomato, red onion, and garlic. To slice avocado in half, run knife around the pit. Twist apart to expose pit. Strike the pit with the blade of a sharp butcher knife and remove. Score avocado meat into small chunks in the peel and remove with a tablespoon. Add to the jalapeño, onion, and garlic. Season with salt, pepper, cumin, and paprika. Add juice of one lemon, harissa, and chopped cilantro. Using a fork, lightly mash avocado and stir to combine. If you would prefer a smoother guacamole, put mixture in a food processor and purée to your liking.

Grilled Corn and Black Bean Salsa

While there are a number of commercially sold fresh salsas that are quite good, why not make one from scratch with fresh ingredients? I guarantee the flavor will be better and your guests will appreciate the extra effort you went to. Remember, in general, corn chips are suitable for a gluten-free lifestyle. However, some commercial brands are made with wheat. Make sure you read the label to be on the safe side. A good brand to use if you can find it is Tostitos Blue Corn Tortilla Chips. I am quite fond of the blue color, and I think the flavor is better than most.

YIELDS APPROXIMATELY 8 SERVINGS

2 large red tomatoes, diced

2 large yellow tomatoes, diced

2 ears corn, grilled, kernels removed from cob

1 can black beans, drained and rinsed

3 jalapeños, roasted, peeled and minced

½ red onion, diced, or 3-4 scallions, diced

4 garlic cloves, minced

¼ cup cilantro, chopped

2 tsp harissa or pinch of crushed red pepper flakes

2 tsp ground cumin

2 tsp Hungarian smoked hot paprika

Kosher salt and freshly ground pepper

3-4 Tbsp lemon juice or lime juice

Toss all ingredients to combine and allow salsa to marinate for at least one hour before serving.

To roast jalapeños
You can either roast over an open flame if you have a gas stove, or you can place jalapeños in an oven at 375 degrees for approximately 25-30 minutes, rotating to char the pepper evenly.

Albóndigas Soup

This is a traditional meatball soup, not unlike an Italian Wedding Soup. My husband happens to love this one and always tries to order it at any Mexican restaurant we go to. Unfortunately not a lot of restaurants have it, and the ones that do have very little meatball and a ton of potato as filler. I prefer this recipe because it is loaded with veggies and meatballs. The vinegar at the end helps to balance the heat of the jalapeños beautifully.

YIELDS APPROXIMATELY 8 SERVINGS

For the meatballs
- ¼ cup olive oil
- 8 garlic cloves, minced
- 2 bunches cilantro, finely minced
- Pinch kosher salt and freshly ground pepper
- 1 lb ground pork
- 1 large egg, beaten
- 1 tsp ground cumin
- 1 tsp Hungarian smoked hot paprika
- Pinch cayenne pepper
- ⅔ cup almond or pecan meal

For the soup
- 3 Tbsp vegetable oil
- 1 leek, washed and finely chopped
- 3 garlic cloves, minced
- 4 carrots, peeled and diced
- ½ head green cabbage, sliced
- 1 jalapeño, stems and seeds removed, minced
- 3 Roma tomatoes, diced
- ½ cup dry sherry or dry vermouth
- 2 tsp ground cumin
- 2 tsp paprika
- Pinch cayenne pepper
- 1 bay leaf
- Pinch kosher salt and freshly ground pepper
- 8 cups Kitchen Basics, Pacifica, or Progresso chicken broth
- 2 Tbsp cilantro, minced
- 3-4 Tbsp white wine vinegar

Combine olive oil, garlic, cilantro, salt, pepper, pork, egg, cumin, paprika, cayenne, and nut meal. Using your hands, gently knead ingredients together until well combined. Form into 1" meatballs. Refrigerate meatballs at least one hour before cooking. Heat the vegetable oil in a large soup pot over medium-high heat. Brown meatballs on all sides, taking care not to rip the meatballs. Remove to a baking sheet.

Add leek to pot and sauté for a minute or two until it begins to become tender. Add garlic and continue sautéing for an additional minute or until fragrant. Add carrots, cabbage, jalapeño, and tomato. Season with salt, pepper, cumin, paprika, cayenne, and bay leaf. Sauté for an additional minute to toast the spices. Deglaze the pan with the sherry, scraping any of the caramelized bits off the bottom of the pan. Continue cooking uncovered until most of the liquid has evaporated. Return meatballs and add chicken broth. Bring to a boil. Cover and reduce heat to a simmer. Cook covered for approximately 45 minutes or until all the vegetables are tender. Add vinegar and cilantro and season to taste. Serve hot.

Pork or Beef Taquitos

Taquitos are a great recipe to make when you have leftover pork or beef roast. I tend to prefer cuts of meat that have more fat on them like pork butt or rump roast. A simple way to prepare the meat is to place in a crock pot with carrots, onions, celery, salt, pepper, paprika, garlic powder, and some cumin. Cover with water or broth and let it simmer away all day until the roast is falling apart. Eat some for dinner and then save the rest for taquitos the next day.

YIELDS APPROXIMATELY 8 SERVINGS

1 lb cooked beef or pork, shredded
16 corn tortillas (Most are gluten-free, but check labels to be sure. Azteca is a good brand)
1 onion, chopped
2 Tbsp vegetable or canola oil
3-4 garlic cloves, minced
Pinch kosher salt and freshly ground pepper

1-2 chipotles in adobo sauce, chopped (La Costeña is a safe brand but check others; most should be safe)
¼ cup red wine vinegar
¼ cup fresh cilantro
1 cup pepper jack cheese, shredded (Don't buy pre-shredded cheese, as it is often coated to keep it from sticking.)
Vegetable oil for frying

Heat tortillas according to package directions and cover with a towel. Heat oil in medium sauté pan over medium-high heat. Add onion and sauté until translucent. Add garlic and sauté for 1 minute or until fragrant. Add pork or beef and sauté for a couple minutes or until the meat begins to brown. Add vinegar, chipotles, salt, pepper, and cilantro and sauté for 1 minute. Season to taste. Place 2 Tbsp of filling on each tortilla and top with cheese. Roll tortillas and secure with a toothpick. Place vegetable oil in a large skillet and heat to 350 degrees. (Either use a thermometer to check temperature of the oil or test it by splashing a bit of water into the oil. It should bubble furiously. Stand back, though, so you don't get burned.) Fry taquitos until golden brown, approximately 2-3 minutes per side. Serve hot with guacamole, grilled corn and black bean salsa, and Daisy sour cream.

Flan

The great debate is flan or crème brulée. They are both custards with a caramel of sorts. I prefer crème brulée with the contrast of the crunchy burnt sugar on top, while my husband prefers flan with its more tender custard and the liquidy caramel on top. Either way, they are both delicious. Please note: caramel is perhaps one of the most dangerous things to work with in the kitchen. If it gets on your skin, it will scorch immediately. Be very cautious while swirling the caramel around the ramekins.

YIELDS 8 SERVINGS

1 cup + ½ cup sugar
6 large eggs
1 14-oz can sweetened condensed milk
1 12-oz can evaporated milk

1 tsp ground cinnamon
1 tsp pure vanilla extract
1 Tbsp orange blossom water

Preheat oven to 325 degrees. Place 1 cup sugar in a small saucepan and heat over medium-high heat until the sugar has melted and turned to caramel. Divide caramel evenly amongst 8 1-cup ramekins, swirling the caramel around the bottom of each ramekin.

Beat eggs, milks, ½ cup sugar, cinnamon, vanilla, and orange blossom water with an immersion blender until well combined. Strain mixture into a large measuring cup. Pour evenly amongst ramekins. Place ramekins in a large glass Pyrex baking dish and pour approximately 1" hot water into baking dish to create hot water bath. Bake for approximately 45 minutes to 1 hour or until the custard is just set. Cool for 1 hour and place in the refrigerator for at least 2 hours before serving.

To serve, remove from refrigerator at least 30 minutes before serving. Using a paring knife, score edges of custard. Invert onto plate. Gently heat with a blow torch, a little at a time so as not to shatter the glass ramekin, until the custard releases from the ramekin. You may need to rescore the edges of the custard a second time to get the custard to release.

Indian
Feast

I ndian cuisine is one of those great culinary traditions that takes advantage of spices to add flavor without adding other fillers or preservatives. As a result it easily lends itself to a gluten-free lifestyle.

Cucumber Raita

This dish is a lot like a traditional Greek tzatziki. It pairs particularly well with spicy dishes as a means of cooling them down. It is also a great alternative to mayonnaise for a sandwich.

Yields 8 Servings

1 large English cucumber, peeled, quartered, seeded, and diced
16 oz plain Fage yogurt
Kosher salt and freshly ground pepper
2 tsp Hungarian smoked hot paprika

2 tsp ground cumin
1 pint grape tomatoes, halved
2 Tbsp lemon juice
2 tsp dried dillweed
1 Tbsp fresh peppermint, minced

Lightly salt the cucumber and place in a colander lined with paper towels. Allow to stand for at least 30 minutes before using, to remove some of the liquid. Place drained cucumbers in a bowl with yogurt, lemon juice, pepper, paprika, cumin, tomatoes, dill, and peppermint. Toss to combine, adjusting seasoning to taste.

Carrot Raita

This is a savory cousin to a very traditional Moroccan salad with shredded carrots, cinnamon, orange blossom water, and argan oil. Again, the cool refreshing crunch of this salad is a perfect accompaniment to a spicy main dish.

YIELDS APPROXIMATELY 8 SERVINGS

¼ cup raisins
½ cup apple cider, hot
16 oz plain Fage yogurt
Kosher salt and freshly ground pepper
2-3 tsp honey, or to taste
1 tsp Hungarian smoked hot paprika

1 tsp ground cumin
1 tsp harissa
3 carrots, peeled and shredded in a food processor
2 Tbsp lemon juice, or to taste

Place raisins in a small bowl and cover with hot cider. Allow to sit for 30 minutes to plump up raisins. Drain. Place in a larger bowl and add yogurt, salt, pepper, honey, paprika, cumin, harissa, carrots, and lemon juice. Toss to combine. Adjust seasoning to taste.

Chicken Tikka Masala

Tikka stands for this specific type of chicken dish but also for the dot that is often seen on Indian foreheads. The dish is traditionally prepared with chicken breast, but I prefer the thigh as it has much more flavor in it.

YIELDS APPROXIMATELY 8 SERVINGS

For the chicken marinade
2 lbs boneless, skinless chicken thighs
Kosher salt and freshly ground pepper

3 Tbsp lemon juice
2 tsp ground ginger
3-4 garlic cloves, minced
2 tsp ground cumin

1 tsp garam masala (a spice blend typical of India. You can find a good one at www.zamourispices.com.)
1 tsp harissa
2 tsp Hungarian smoked hot paprika
2 Tbsp extra virgin olive oil (Not typical to India but I prefer it for cooking.)

Place all the ingredients in a bowl. Toss to combine. Cover with plastic wrap and place in the refrigerator to marinate overnight. Remove from the refrigerator approximately 30 minutes before cooking.

For the stew
2 Tbsp extra virgin olive oil
1 large onion, quartered and sliced
1 Tbsp fresh ginger, peeled and minced
4 garlic cloves, minced
2 tsp ground coriander
Pinch saffron
1 tsp harissa
2 tsp Hungarian smoked hot paprika
¼ cup plain Fage yogurt
1 14-oz can fire-roasted tomatoes, diced
2 cups Kitchen Basics, Pacifica, or Progresso chicken broth
Kosher salt and freshly ground pepper
½ tsp garam masala
¼ cup cilantro, minced
¼ cup mint leaves, minced

Heat oil in a large sauté pan. Add chicken and sauté for approximately 5 minutes until the chicken begins to brown. Add onions and sauté until they begin to get golden brown. Add garlic and ginger and sauté for 1 minute or until fragrant. Add coriander, saffron, harissa, paprika, salt, pepper, and garam masala and sauté for 1 minute to toast the spices. Add tomatoes and chicken broth. Bring to a boil and reduce heat to a simmer. Simmer covered for approximately 45 minutes or until the chicken is tender. Add yogurt, cilantro, and mint and heat through. Adjust seasoning to taste. Serve with steamed basmati rice.

Indian Spiced Rice Pudding

I actually made this recipe for the first time for a vegan. I knew I couldn't use butter or milk so I had to come up with an alternative for her. I had used almond milk with great results for other desserts so I decided to try it. The dish ended up turning out so well I decided to make it with almond milk permanently. About 3 days later I had a gluten-free guest who came with a group for dinner, and I gave him the same dessert. He emailed me about 2 days later asking me for the recipe because he loved it, too. So here it is!

YIELDS 8 SERVINGS

2 cups cooked basmati rice
1 can coconut milk
1 cup almond milk
½-¾ cup pure maple syrup
1 tsp pure vanilla extract
1 tsp ground cinnamon
Pinch ground cloves
1 tsp ground cardamom
1 tsp ground ginger
Pinch freshly grated nutmeg
½ cup dried cranberries
½ cup toasted pistachios

Heat almond milk and cooled rice in a medium saucepan. Stir until milk is heated through and the rice begins to thicken. Add coconut milk, vanilla, and spices. Continue stirring on medium-high heat until the pudding is thickened. Remove from heat and add syrup to sweeten to taste. Cool slightly. Add pistachios and cranberries. Scoop into 8 custard cups. Cover with plastic wrap and place in the refrigerator for approximately 3 hours before serving.

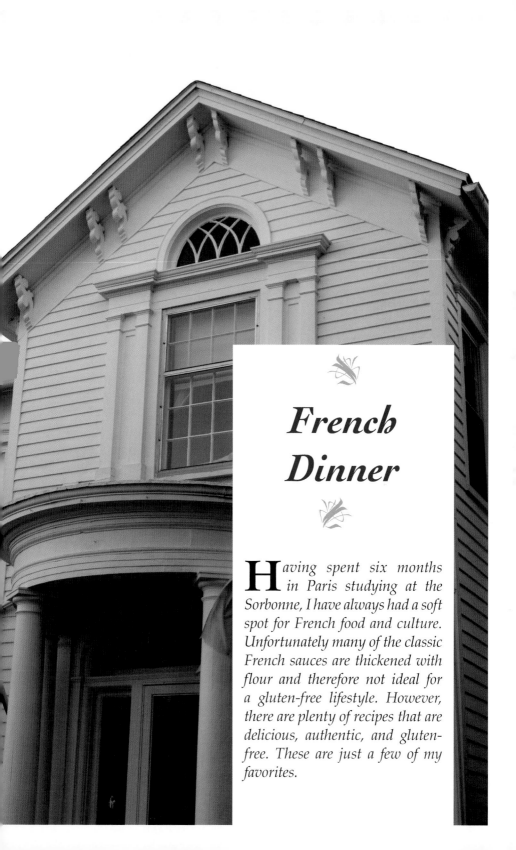

French Dinner

Having spent six months in Paris studying at the Sorbonne, I have always had a soft spot for French food and culture. Unfortunately many of the classic French sauces are thickened with flour and therefore not ideal for a gluten-free lifestyle. However, there are plenty of recipes that are delicious, authentic, and gluten-free. These are just a few of my favorites.

Potato Leek Soup

A quintessential French classic. The chilled version of this soup is called vichyssoise. You can take this recipe and chill it to serve or serve it hot with some homemade crème fraîche. Either way your guests will probably want seconds.

YIELDS APPROXIMATELY 6-8 SERVINGS

*4 oz pancetta
(In France they use lardons, a very fatty bacon-like cut that is difficult to find in the U.S. except perhaps in bigger cities where you may find more specialty gourmet markets.)
2-3 Tbsp extra virgin olive oil
3 leeks, washed and sliced
3 medium russet or Kennebec potatoes, peeled and diced*

*2-3 garlic cloves
2 carrots, peeled and diced
2 celery stalks, diced
1 bay leaf
Kosher salt and freshly ground pepper
2 tsp herbes de Provence
1 tsp Hungarian hot paprika
½ cup dry vermouth or dry sherry
4-6 cups chicken broth
¼-½ cup sour cream*

To clean the leeks, cut off both ends and slice the leeks in half lengthwise. Then place in a bowl and cover with water. Let soak for approximately 15 minutes. This will remove any remaining sand or silt that has gotten caught between the layers.

Heat olive oil in a stockpot over medium-high heat. Add chopped pancetta and sauté until crispy and golden brown. Add leeks and cook until leeks are tender, approximately 3-4 minutes. Add garlic and sauté for 1 minute or until fragrant. Add carrots and celery and sauté for 3 minutes or until they begin to soften. Add potatoes and spices and sauté for 1 minute to toast the spices. Add vermouth and bring to a boil. Cook on high until all the liquid has evaporated. Add chicken broth and bring to a boil. Simmer covered for approximately 45 minutes. Remove bay leaves and purée soup with an immersion blender. Add sour cream and purée again to incorporate. Adjust seasoning with salt and pepper to taste.

Homemade Crème Fraîche

⅔ cups sour cream
⅓ cup heavy cream

Whisk to combine and allow to sit in the refrigerator for approximately 2 hours before using. Will keep for up to one week in the refrigerator.

Mixed Greens with Chèvre, Candied Pecans, Pear, and Champagne Wine Vinaigrette

To really serve this the French way, save the salad course for after the entrée as a palate cleanser before the dessert. According to the French, this actually helps with digestion. And of course, a salad is really best when you can get good quality fresh greens. Use whatever is in season and make sure you include a good assortment of more buttery and crisp lettuces along with the more peppery or bitter ones.

YIELDS 8 SERVINGS

For the salad

4 cups mixed salad greens

2 Bosc or Bartlett pears, quartered and seeded

4 Tbsp candied pecans (recipe below)

8 oz Chèvre or fresh goat cheese (If you cannot find a good quality imported French Chèvre or MontChèvre, feel free to use a domestic fresh goat cheese. I really like the Capricorn brand which comes from Wisconsin and is available at most grocery stores. Don't buy pre-crumbled cheese. Get a log and crumble it yourself.)

For the dressing

½ cup olive oil

2 Tbsp champagne wine
   vinegar

2 Tbsp dry sherry

2 Tbsp Grey Poupon
   Dijon mustard

2 Tbsp honey

Pinch kosher salt and
   freshly ground pepper

Place olive oil, vinegar, sherry, mustard, and honey in a tightly sealing Tupperware container and season with salt and pepper. Close lid and shake vigorously to combine. (This may seem obvious but some Tupperware seems to be tightly closed until you start shaking salad dressing around and it ends up everywhere. It's a mess to clean up, so find one with a good seal).

Toss the greens with enough dressing to coat the leaves without drowning them. To serve, place the greens nicely in the center of 8 plates and top with 1 oz cheese, 1 Tbsp pecans, and ¼ pear that has been sliced.

Candied Pecans

1 cup pecan halves

¼ cup unsalted butter

Pinch kosher salt

Pinch cayenne pepper

½ tsp ground cinnamon

Pinch ground cloves

Pinch freshly grated
   nutmeg

Pinch ground cardamom

1 tsp pure vanilla extract

¼ cup sugar

Place butter, sugar, and spices in a small saucepan. Melt butter over medium-high heat until the sugar has melted and the spices are incorporated. Toast pecan halves in a toaster oven or the oven on a baking sheet for 10 minutes at 350 degrees. Toss toasted pecans with melted butter mixture and coat well. Allow to sit for 30 minutes to give the spices a chance to adhere to the pecans. Keep in a Ziploc baggie at room temperature for up to 2 weeks.

Coq au Vin

Literally translates to "chicken in wine." The wine in this dish serves a dual purpose. First, it gives the chicken delicious flavor. Second, the acid in the wine acts as a tenderizer to keep the chicken moist. This dish is one that benefits from a little marinating and is even better served reheated the next day, so make plenty for leftovers. Be sure you select a dry red wine, like Bordeaux or Burgundy, that isn't too tannic. Merlot and Cabernet Sauvignon are lovely to drink but aren't ideal for cooking. And don't ever use the "cooking wines" that you find in the vinegar section of your grocery store. These are loaded with sodium and are not fit for drinking. Always select a wine that you would drink.

YIELDS 4 SERVINGS

4 boneless, skinless chicken breasts
¼ cup Domata Living Flour
3 slices bacon, diced
2 Tbsp unsalted butter
1 large onion, chopped
3-4 garlic cloves, minced
1 cup baby carrots
1 lb frozen pearl onions, thawed
1 lb sliced button mushrooms
2-3 Tbsp tomato paste

½ cup port
1½ -2 cups dry red wine
2 cups chicken broth
2 bay leaves
Pinch kosher salt and freshly ground pepper
1 Tbsp herbes de Provence, plus 1 tsp
2 Tbsp unsalted butter
2 Tbsp extra virgin olive oil
Pinch freshly grated nutmeg
¼-½ cup dry vermouth

Dry chicken breasts with a paper towel and dredge lightly in flour. (By drying the chicken you enable it to brown properly). Heat a large skillet over medium-high heat. Add bacon and cook approximately 5 minutes or until the bacon begins to crisp up. Add chicken breasts and brown on both sides, approximately 3 minutes per side. Add onion and cook approximately 5 minutes or until onion becomes tender and translucent. Add garlic and cook 1 minute or until fragrant. Add baby carrots, bay leaves, salt, pepper, 1 Tbsp herbes de Provence, and tomato paste. Cook a couple of minutes just to toast the spices. Deglaze the pan with port. Reduce until most of the liquid has evaporated. Add red wine and broth and bring to a boil. Cover and reduce to a simmer. Cook for 45 minutes or until the chicken is tender, rotating the chicken periodically to cook evenly in the wine. Note: Be sure not to shortchange yourself on time with this dish. It is necessary to cook the rawness out of the wine. As wonderful as wine is to drink, from the second it hits the heat the alcohol has a horrendous taste until it has a chance to burn off and develop its flavor.

In the meantime, heat olive oil and butter in a medium sauté pan over medium-high heat until the butter has melted. Add mushrooms and pearl onions. Season with salt, pepper, 1 tsp herbes de Provence, and a pinch of nutmeg. Add vermouth and turn heat to high. Cook uncovered until all the liquid has evaporated and the mushrooms and onions begin to caramelize. Add mushroom/onion mix to the cooked chicken and bring to a boil. Cook on medium-high heat for a few minutes or until the stew has thickened and become glossy. Season to taste.

Roasted Garlic Mashed Potatoes

Regardless of the menu, this is a fantastic side dish to add to your repertoire. It takes boring everyday mashed potatoes and makes something extraordinary out of them. And don't skimp on the butter. That's what gives the potatoes their wonderful flavor and texture, and of course Julia Child would greatly object at the notion of limiting the butter.

YIELDS APPROXIMATELY 4 SERVINGS

4 large russet or Kennebec potatoes, peeled and chopped into ½" cubes
1 head garlic, outer skins peeled off, roasted*

1 Tbsp olive oil
1 stick unsalted butter
Pinch kosher salt and freshly ground pepper
½-¾ cup heavy cream

Place the peeled and chopped potatoes in a medium saucepan. Cover with water and add a pinch of salt. Bring to a boil and cook for approximately 25-30 minutes or until the potatoes are fork tender. Remove from heat and drain potatoes. Add butter, all the garlic from the head of roasted garlic, a pinch of salt and pepper, and enough cream to make the potatoes smooth. Mash with a potato masher. Adjust seasoning to taste.

Note: Don't ever place potatoes in a food processor to mash; they will become tough and gummy.

*To roast the garlic

Place whole head of garlic on a piece of aluminum foil. Drizzle with olive oil and seal foil tightly around the garlic. Place on a baking sheet and roast in a 350 degree preheated oven for approximately 1 hour. Let cool.

*Relax on the patio and enjoy
the fireflies at twilight at the
Chestnut Street Inn*

Crème Brulée

This is probably the single most frequently ordered dessert in a restaurant. Everyone has a perception that it is difficult and fancy. In reality, there are a few simple tricks to follow to create perfect crème brulée every time. This one has a few special ingredients in it to give it a unique flavor.

YIELDS 8 SERVINGS

4 cups heavy cream
2 tsp vanilla extract
9 egg yolks
¾ cup sugar

1 Tbsp orange blossom
  water
1 tsp ground cinnamon
¼ cup sugar for bruléeing

Preheat oven to 325 degrees.

Place cream, orange blossom water, and vanilla in a heavy saucepan over medium heat. Separate 9 egg yolks from their whites. Whisk the yolks with ¾ cup sugar and cinnamon until sugar is dissolved and the yolks become a paler yellow. Once the cream begins to bubble along the edges, remove from heat and slowly begin pouring the hot cream into the yolk/sugar mix, whisking constantly so that the yolks do not scramble. Once all the cream has been combined, strain the mix through a strainer into a large Pyrex measuring cup, to remove any clumpy bits.

Place 8 1-cup ramekins in a large glass Pyrex baking dish. I prefer deeper custard cups to shallow ones, because it increases the ratio of custard to burnt sugar. I also prefer a glass baking dish to a metal one, as it conducts heat better and will decrease the baking time for your crème brulée.

Pour the cream mixture evenly into 8 ramekins. Fill Pyrex baking dish approximately ⅓ full with boiling water to create a hot water bath around the ramekins. Bake in the oven for approximately 45 minutes or until the custards are just set but still a little wiggly. If the custards begin to brown on top, cover them with aluminum foil until they are set. Do not overbake the custards or they will become gummy. If you underbake them they will not set properly. You are basically looking for a consistency like Jell-O.

Cool the custards for one hour at room temperature and then cover and refrigerate for at least 3 hours. The crème brulée can be made up to 3 days ahead. Before serving, sprinkle the tops of the custards with a thin layer of granulated sugar. Carefully brulée the tops with a commercial blow torch. (Don't bother with the little home versions. They are twice as expensive and not nearly as effective as a commercial blow torch.) You can place the custards under the broiler to brulée the tops—but I find that this doesn't maintain the contrast between the cool custard and the burnt top, but rather heats up the ramekins and the custard in the process.

I guess I'd call this dinner my tribute to Julia Child, as many of the recipes were inspired by the legend. Her birthday is on August 15, an opportune time to host a party in her honor. Make sure you have plenty of wine on hand, just as she would have had it, and top off the evening by showing "Julie and Julia" and clips of her French Chef series.

Gâteau d'Omelettes avec Pipérades et Champignons

Literally translates to "omelette cake with sautéed peppers and mushrooms." I owe this recipe to Julia Child. It was the salad course for my Tribute to Julia Child in 2009. It came from her French Chef series. My version takes some liberties with the mushrooms and the peppers, but the rest is pure Julia. You can assemble the cake in advance and bake it right before serving.

YIELDS APPROXIMATELY 8 SERVINGS

2 Tbsp unsalted butter
½ Vidalia onion, cut into quarters and sliced
½ bell pepper, cut into strips and then each strip cut in half
1 garlic clove, minced
Kosher salt and freshly ground pepper
1 tsp herbes de Provence
¼ cup white wine
1 14-oz can diced tomatoes
2 Tbsp unsalted butter
Kosher salt and freshly ground pepper

8 oz baby bella mushrooms, stems removed, peeled and sliced
1 garlic clove, minced
1 tsp herbes de Provence
Pinch freshly grated nutmeg
¼ cup white wine
8 eggs
8 Tbsp water
Kosher salt and freshly ground pepper
5 Tbsp unsalted butter
1 cup Swiss cheese, shredded
Crème fraîche to garnish

Heat 2 Tbsp butter in small sauté pan over medium-high heat. Once butter has melted, add onions and bell pepper and sauté until the onions begin to caramelize. Add garlic and sauté 1 minute or until fragrant. Add salt, pepper, and herbes de Provence. Deglaze pan with ¼ cup white wine. Continue cooking until most of the liquid is reduced. Add tomatoes and cook until all the liquid has evaporated, stirring occasionally. Remove from heat and adjust seasoning to taste. Transfer to another bowl to cool.

In same pan, add 2 Tbsp butter and return to heat. Once butter has melted, add garlic and sauté until fragrant, 1 minute. Add mushrooms and toss gently. Add salt, pepper, herbes de Provence, and nutmeg. Deglaze pan with ¼ cup white wine. Continue cooking on high, tossing occasionally, until all the liquid has evaporated and the mushrooms begin to brown lightly. Adjust seasoning to taste and remove to another bowl to cool.

In a separate bowl, whisk together eggs and water and season with salt and pepper. Heat 1 Tbsp butter in same sauté pan over medium-high heat until the butter has melted and stopped bubbling, but isn't brown. Add one ladle of egg mixture. Allow to set for a few seconds and gently swirl pan to distribute egg mixture evenly in pan. Allow to cook another couple of seconds until just set.

Remove omelette to baking dish. Layer with ⅓ of bell pepper mixture. Make another omelette and layer over bell peppers. Add ⅓ mushrooms. Repeat omelette and layer over mushrooms. Add another ⅓ peppers. Repeat omelette and layer over peppers. Add remaining mushrooms. Make last omelette with remaining eggs and layer on top of mushrooms. Top with remaining peppers. Top entire "cake" with shredded Swiss cheese. Can be made in advance up to this point. Bake in 350 degree oven for approximately 10 minutes or until cheese is melted, bubbling, and begins to brown on top. Remove from oven and cut into 8 pie wedges. Serve each wedge with homemade crème fraîche.

Gâteau d'Omelettes avec
Pipérades et Champignons
(recipe on previous page)

Herb Roasted Potatoes

Another very basic side dish to add to the repertoire, this pairs well with almost any dinner. You can use red potatoes, baby Dutch potatoes, Fingerling potatoes, or even a Yukon Gold that has been cut into 1" pieces. For the smaller potatoes, leave them whole.

YIELDS 6-8 SERVINGS

1 lb roasting potatoes, cut in half
3 Tbsp extra virgin olive oil
Kosher salt and freshly ground pepper

2 tsp garlic powder
2 tsp Hungarian smoked hot paprika
2-3 tsp herbes de Provence

Place potatoes on a baking sheet. Drizzle with olive oil and season with salt, pepper, garlic powder, paprika, and herbes de Provence. Toss to coat evenly. Spread potatoes out in a single layer, cut side up. Roast in a 375 degree oven for approximately 45 minutes or until puffy and golden.

Spinach Salad with Warm Bacon Vinaigrette

Practically perfect in every way, to quote Mary Poppins. The tender young spinach leaves just barely begin to wilt with the heat of the bacon fat. Be sure to serve this salad immediately. It just isn't the same once the spinach is totally wilted and the bacon fat is cold.

YIELDS 6 SERVINGS

3 eggs
1 lb baby spinach leaves
1 tsp sugar
6 Tbsp apple cider vinegar
2 sliced shallots

Pinch kosher salt and
    freshly ground pepper
2 garlic cloves, minced
8 slices applewood
    smoked bacon, chopped

Place eggs in saucepan and cover with cold water and a pinch of salt. Bring to a boil and cook for 10 minutes. Rinse under cold water and let cool. Peel eggs and cut into slices with an egg slicer. Cook bacon in a sauté pan until crisp. Remove bacon from pan and drain on paper towels. Do not discard the bacon fat. Combine vinegar with sugar, salt, and pepper. Sauté shallots in bacon fat until golden, approximately 3 minutes. Add garlic and cook for 1 minute until fragrant. Add vinegar/sugar mix and bring to a boil. Cook for 1 minute and remove from heat. Pour hot dressing over spinach leaves and toss quickly so the leaves do not wilt. Distribute amongst 6 plates and serve with one half of an egg per plate and a sprinkle of the cooked bacon bits.

Boeuf Bourguignon

Literally translated as "Beef Burgundy," this dish was originally named for the Burgundy wine it was cooked in. For anyone who saw the 2009 movie "Julie and Julia" starring Meryl Streep as the legendary Julia Child, you will remember this as the dish Julie Powell made for editor Judith Jones. After the movie came out, this was a hot selection for dinner parties at the inn. I could practically make it in my sleep, although I wouldn't advise doing so.

1½ lb filet tips
2-3 Tbsp Domata Living
  Flour
6-8 slices applewood
  smoked bacon, chopped
1 large onion, chopped
3-4 garlic cloves, minced
1 cup baby carrots
2 Tbsp unsalted butter
1 Tbsp extra virgin olive oil
1 lb frozen pearl onions,
  thawed
1 lb sliced button
  mushrooms
3 Tbsp tomato paste

½ cup port
1½-2 cups dry red wine,
  Bordeaux or Burgundy
2 cups Kitchen Basics,
  Pacifica, or Progresso
  beef broth
2 bay leaves
Pinch kosher salt and
  freshly ground pepper
2 Tbsp herbes de
  Provence, plus 1 tsp
Pinch freshly grated
  nutmeg
¼ cup dry vermouth or
  dry sherry

Pat filet tips dry with a paper towel. Coat lightly in flour. Cook bacon in medium stockpot over medium-high heat until lightly browned and fat has rendered out. Push bacon to sides of pan. Add beef and brown on all sides, approximately 5 minutes. Add onion and cook 5 minutes or until translucent. Add garlic and cook 1 minute or until fragrant. Add baby carrots, bay leaves, salt, pepper, 2 Tbsp herbes de Provence, and tomato paste. Cook a couple of minutes to toast the spices. Add port and bring to a boil. Simmer until almost all liquid evaporates. Add red wine and beef broth, just to halfway up the pan. Bring to a boil. Cover and simmer on low for 1½ hours or until beef is tender. Meanwhile, heat olive oil and butter in a medium sauté pan over medium-high heat until the butter has melted. Add mushrooms and pearl onions. Season with salt, pepper, 1 tsp herbes de Provence, and a pinch of nutmeg. Add vermouth or sherry and bring to a boil. Simmer on medium-high heat, uncovered, until all the liquid has evaporated and the mushrooms and onions begin to caramelize. Add mushroom/onion mix to the cooked beef and bring to a boil. Cook on medium-high heat for a few minutes or until the stew has thickened and become glossy. Season to taste.

Chocolate Espresso Pots de Crème

Like the sweet potato pots de crème, this custard is almost like a cross between a chocolate mousse and a chocolate crème brulée. As it bakes, it forms several layers: a top skin, a center chocolate layer, and the bottom creamy layer. It is complex and delicious.

YIELDS 6 SERVINGS

6 egg yolks
2 Tbsp sugar
6 oz semi-sweet chocolate
2 tsp instant coffee or 1
 Tbsp brewed coffee

1 tsp pure vanilla extract
⅓ cup heavy cream
1⅓ cup whole milk
1 Tbsp ChocoVine
Pinch kosher salt

Preheat oven to 300 degrees.

Place chocolate chips, coffee, vanilla extract, cream, milk, and ChocoVine in a medium saucepan over medium heat. Whisk until all the chocolate has melted and the cream/milk is hot but not boiling. Remove from heat and let cool for a couple of minutes. In a medium mixing bowl, beat egg yolks along with 2 Tbsp sugar and salt until the yolks are pale and creamy. Slowly whisk in the melted chocolate/cream mixture, being careful not to scramble the egg yolks. Strain custard mix into a large measuring cup.

Place 6 1-cup glass ramekins in a large Pyrex baking dish. Distribute custard batter into the ramekins equally. Pour boiling water into the baking dish, creating a hot water bath for the custards to bake in. Bake for approximately 35-40 minutes or until the custards are just set, but still a bit jiggly, like Jell-O. Remove from the oven and let custards cool for approximately one hour before covering each ramekin with plastic wrap and placing in the refrigerator. Chill for at least 3 hours before serving. Serve dusted with powdered sugar and garnished with either fresh raspberries or fresh blueberries.

Soup Party

Whether you serve it for lunch, a first course, or as a full dinner, soup is always one of my favorite foods, not only to eat, but especially to make. A really good soup requires time and careful layering of flavors. I prefer my soups puréed the French way over chunky. And all of these soups freeze beautifully, so you can always have homemade soup on hand. Forget the stuff out of the can that's usually high in sodium, high in fat, and low in flavor.

Egyptian Red Lentil Soup

Perhaps one of the more unusual soups that I make, this soup always surprises everyone with its lemony zing, spicy heat, and bold flavor. Red lentils are generally available at most specialty markets or ethnic grocers. They are different from other lentils not only in color, but in texture. Less starchy, they lend themselves to this soup much better than their green or brown cousins. Note: Saffron is considered to be the most expensive commodity on the planet by weight. It is the stamen of a crocus flower. Because it is so fragile, it has to be harvested very gently by hand with tweezers; hence the high price. It is a very unique flavor that cannot be substituted. If you choose to leave it out because of price, that is understandable, but there is nothing to replace it, especially not turmeric, which is very strong in flavor and will overpower the dish.

YIELDS APPROXIMATELY 8-10 SERVINGS

3 Tbsp extra virgin olive oil
1 red onion, chopped
3 garlic cloves, minced
2 carrots, peeled and diced
2 celery stalks, diced
1½ cups red lentils
6 cups Kitchen Basics, Pacifica, or Progresso chicken broth

Kosher salt and freshly ground pepper
Pinch saffron
2 tsp ground cumin
2 tsp Hungarian smoked hot paprika
2 tsp harissa
3 Tbsp chopped Italian parsley
3 Tbsp chopped cilantro
½ to ¾ cup lemon juice

Heat oil in a stockpot. Add onions and sauté until tender, approximately 5 minutes. Add garlic and sauté for 1 minute or until fragrant. Add carrots, celery, and spices, including harissa, and stir to combine. Cook for a couple minutes to toast spices. Add lentils, parsley, cilantro, and chicken broth. Bring to a boil. Simmer on low for approximately 40 minutes. Purée soup with an immersion blender. Add lemon juice to taste. Adjust seasonings to taste.

Cream of Mushroom Soup

Mushrooms are one of those ingredients that garner much debate. Many people don't like them because of their texture. They feel that they are mushy. Puréeing the mushrooms into a soup eliminates the texture debate. I like to use an assortment of mushrooms for maximum flavor. Reminder: Never wash mushrooms or they will become waterlogged. Always either wipe them clean with a damp cloth or peel them by removing the stems and lifting away the outer skin. If you do not find a good assortment of fresh mushrooms, you can use dehydrated mushrooms. Simply cover them in hot water for approximately 20 minutes to rehydrate. Chop and use the same way you would a fresh mushroom. To really boost the mushroom flavor, use the reserved liquid that you rehydrated the mushrooms with in addition to the chicken stock in the soup.

YIELDS APPROXIMATELY 6-8 SERVINGS

2 lbs assorted mushrooms (a combo of any mushrooms you can find)
2 Tbsp extra virgin olive oil
1 Tbsp unsalted butter
2 carrots, peeled and diced
2 celery sticks, diced
1 large sweet onion, Vidalia or Walla Walla, diced
2-3 garlic cloves, minced
½ cup dry sherry or dry vermouth

4 cups Kitchen Basics, Pacifica, or Progresso chicken broth
Pinch kosher salt and freshly ground pepper
Pinch freshly grated nutmeg
2 tsp Hungarian smoked hot paprika
2 Tbsp herbes de Provence
2 bay leaves
½ cup Daisy sour cream
2 tsp white truffle oil

In a large stockpot over medium-high heat, heat olive oil and butter until the butter has melted. Add the onions and cook until they become translucent, approximately 5 minutes. Add garlic and cook for an additional minute until fragrant. Add celery and carrots and cook for a couple minutes or until the vegetables begin to soften. Add mushrooms. Season with salt, pepper, nutmeg, paprika, herbes de Provence, and bay leaves. Deglaze the pan with sherry or vermouth and turn heat to high. Cook uncovered on high heat until all the liquid has evaporated and the mushrooms begin to caramelize. Add stock. Bring to a boil, cover, and cook for approximately 30 minutes or until all the vegetables are cooked through. Remove the bay leaves. Purée soup with an immersion blender until practically smooth. Add sour cream and purée again to incorporate the sour cream. Add truffle oil and adjust seasoning to taste. Serve hot, garnished with homemade crème fraîche.

Roasted Butternut Squash Soup

This is arguably my most popular soup. It is really best made in the fall, when butternut squash is in season and at the peak of its ripeness. You want a squash that isn't too starchy and doesn't have a lot of seeds. Smaller ones tend to be sweeter. You can knock on the skin of a butternut, and if the squash sounds hollow, there are a lot of seeds. By roasting rather than boiling the squash, you draw out the natural sugars of the squash, giving it a nutty caramel flavor that makes this soup entirely unique. The roasted squash is also a delicious side dish as-is, without making it into a soup.

YIELDS APPROXIMATELY 8-10 SERVINGS

For the roasted squash

2 small butternut squashes
2 medium onions, chopped
2 medium carrots, peeled and chopped
2 celery stalks, chopped
2 garlic cloves, minced
2 Tbsp extra virgin olive oil

1 tsp kosher salt
½ tsp freshly ground pepper
1 tsp Hungarian smoked hot paprika
1 Tbsp herbes de Provence

For the soup stock

2 Tbsp extra virgin olive oil
2 Tbsp unsalted butter
2 tsp kosher salt
½ tsp freshly ground
  pepper
Pinch freshly grated nutmeg
1 tsp Hungarian smoked
  hot paprika

2 bay leaves
1 Tbsp herbes de Provence
½ cup dry vermouth or
  dry sherry
7 cups Kitchen Basics,
  Pacifica, or Progresso
  chicken broth
½-¾ cup Daisy sour
  cream

Preheat oven to 375 degrees.

Cut off both ends of each butternut squash. Using a strong vegetable peeler, peel the squash. Cut in half lengthwise and scoop out the seeds, using a spoon. Cut squash into approximately 1" pieces and put on a baking sheet. Drizzle with 2 Tbsp olive oil, 1 tsp salt, ½ tsp pepper, 1 tsp paprika, 1 Tbsp herbes de Provence. Using your hands, toss the squash in oil and seasonings and spread out onto baking sheet in a single layer. Roast the butternut squash approximately 55 minutes or until tender.

In a medium stockpot over medium-high heat, add remaining 2 Tbsp olive oil and butter. Once the butter has melted, add onions and sauté until tender, approximately 5 minutes. Add garlic and sauté 1 minute until fragrant. Add carrots and celery and remaining spices and sauté approximately 5 minutes more. Add the roasted butternut squash and then the ½ cup vermouth or sherry. Bring heat to high and reduce the liquid until most of it has evaporated. Add chicken stock and bring to a boil. Cover and reduce heat to a simmer. Simmer covered for 45 minutes. Turn off heat and remove bay leaves. Using an immersion blender, purée the soup until creamy. Add sour cream and purée until the sour cream is well incorporated. Adjust seasoning to taste. Serve hot with a dollop of homemade crème fraîche.

Gluten-Free Beer and Cheese Soup

There was a time when beer was off limits for those who needed a gluten-free diet. Not anymore. A number of gluten-free beers have now surfaced. Good ones for use in this soup are Honey Beer, Pioneer Lager, and Green's Quest Tripel Blonde Ale. Most grocery stores and liquor stores now carry at least one gluten-free beer option. You want to use one that isn't too dark or too bitter, or it will overpower the soup. For a great list of gluten-free beers, google the article "Celiacs Guide to Gluten Free Beer" by Carolyn Smagalski.

YIELDS APPROXIMATELY 8 SERVINGS

3 slices applewood
   smoked bacon, cut into
   chunks
1 onion, diced
3-4 garlic cloves, minced
2 carrots, peeled and diced
2 celery stalks, diced
2 large russett or
   Kennebec potatoes,
   peeled and diced
Pinch kosher salt and
   freshly ground pepper

1 tsp Hungarian smoked
   hot paprika
2 bay leaves
2 Tbsp herbes de Provence
1 bottle gluten-free beer
4 cups Kitchen Basics,
   Pacifica, or Progresso
   chicken broth
½-¾ cup Daisy sour
   cream
1 cup aged cheddar cheese,
   grated

Cook bacon in a medium stockpot over medium heat. Remove to paper towels to drain. Add onion to bacon fat and sauté until translucent, approximately 5 minutes. Add garlic and sauté until fragrant, approximately 1 minute. Add carrots, celery, and potato and sauté for an additional couple of minutes. Add spices and heat for 1 minute. Add beer. Bring to a boil and cook, uncovered, until all the liquid has evaporated. Add chicken broth and bring to a boil. Cover and simmer on low for 45 minutes. Remove bay leaves and purée with an immersion blender. Add sour cream and cheese and purée until smooth. Season to taste with salt and pepper. Serve with reserved bacon pieces and a dollop of homemade crème fraîche.

Here are just a few more great soup recipes that I couldn't resist including.

Harira

Harira is a traditional Moroccan soup that is generally served during the month of Ramadan. Most Moroccans will eat a hot bowl of the soup first thing at sundown, along with a few dates, to break their fast. It is hearty, filling, and full of nutrition.

YIELDS APPROXIMATELY 8 SERVINGS

1 lb beef stew meat
2-3 Tbsp extra virgin olive oil
2 large onions, chopped
2-3 garlic cloves, minced
1 can chickpeas, drained
½ cup lentils, rinsed and drained
1 24-oz can whole peeled tomatoes, crushed
4 stalks celery, diced
2 carrots, peeled and diced
1 Tbsp tomato paste

Pinch kosher salt and freshly ground pepper
1 tsp ground ginger
½ tsp saffron
2-3 tsp ras el hanout
2 tsp harissa
½ cup basmati rice
1 bunch chopped cilantro
1 bunch chopped Italian parsley
8 cups Kitchen Basics, Pacifica, or Progresso beef broth

Heat olive oil in a large stockpot over medium-high heat. Add beef and brown on all sides. Add onions and sauté about 5 minutes or until onions begin to soften and turn translucent. Add garlic and cook 1 minute or until fragrant. Add celery and carrots and sauté 5 minutes or until they begin to soften. Add lentils, tomato paste, tomatoes, harissa, and spices. Add beef broth and bring to a boil. Cover and reduce to a simmer. Cook for 1 to 1½ hours or until beef is very tender, adding liquid as needed. Add rice, cilantro, parsley, and chickpeas and bring to a boil. Cover and reduce to a simmer. Cook 20 minutes or until rice is cooked through. Adjust seasoning to taste.

Crab or Shrimp Bisque

Seafood bisques and chowders are extremely popular. This recipe can be made with either shrimp or crab. Be sure to use good quality lump crab. You can actually find canned lump crab which is a little less expensive than going to your seafood counter and is generally fresher than what they call "fresh" seafood. All seafood gets to a grocery store frozen, not thawed. If you prefer to buy it over the counter, request the seafood that is still frozen and thaw it when you are ready to use it. For shrimp, be sure to purchase shrimp that has already been peeled and deveined. It's a nasty thing to have to do yourself.

YIELDS APPROXIMATELY 8 SERVINGS

2 Tbsp extra virgin olive oil
2 Tbsp unsalted butter
6-8 green onions, sliced
3-4 garlic cloves, minced
3 carrots, peeled and diced
3 celery stalks, diced
3 parsnips, peeled and diced
1 6-oz can tomato paste
3 4-oz cans lump crab meat, drained, or 1 lb shrimp
½ cup champagne or sparkling wine
Kosher salt and freshly ground pepper
1 tsp harissa
2 bay leaves
2-3 tsp Hungarian smoked hot paprika
2 Tbsp herbes de Provence
2 jars clam juice
4 cups Kitchen Basics, Pacifica, or Progresso chicken broth
½-¾ cup Daisy sour cream
1 4-oz can lump crab, drained, or 1 cup cooked shrimp to garnish

Heat oil and butter in a large stockpot over medium-high heat. Add onions and sauté for 2-3 minutes or until softened. Add garlic and sauté for 1 minute until fragrant. Add carrots, celery, parsnips, tomato paste, and crab or shrimp. Sauté for 1 minute to combine. Add salt, pepper, harissa, bay leaves, paprika, and herbes de Provence. Sauté for 1 minute to toast the spices. Add champagne or sparkling wine and bring to a boil. Cook on high, uncovered, until all the liquid has evaporated. Add clam juice and chicken broth. Bring to a boil. Cover and reduce heat to a simmer. Cook for approximately 45 minutes. Remove bay leaves and purée with an immersion blender. Add sour cream and purée to combine. Adjust seasoning to taste. Serve hot with dollop of crème fraîche and top with either crab meat or cooked shrimp, respectively.

Spicy Tomato and Chocolate Soup

I invented this recipe for an annual chocolate dinner we host. All the courses involve chocolate, but with a savory application. Historically speaking, chocolate was used in Mayan and Aztec culture as a means of cutting the heat of chili peppers. It was also considered medicinal and often made into a hot beverage as a cure for various ailments. The chocolate should be prevalent, but not overpowering. Depending upon the chocolate you use, you may have to adjust the amount to get the right ratio of chocolate to heat. "Queso fresco" literally translates to "fresh cheese." It is a mild, easily crumbled cheese that works wonderful as a neutral creamy garnish on this soup. If you can't find it, use goat cheese or simply crème fraîche to cut the heat.

YIELDS APPROXIMATELY 6-8 SERVINGS

2 Tbsp extra virgin olive oil

2 Tbsp unsalted butter

1 onion, diced

3 garlic cloves, minced

2 carrots, peeled and diced

2 celery stalks, diced

1 cup sun-dried tomatoes, sliced

Kosher salt and freshly ground pepper

3 Tbsp harissa

2 tsp Hungarian hot paprika

2 tsp ground cumin

1 tsp ground coriander

½-¾ cup dry sherry or white wine

1 28-oz can diced tomatoes

4 cups Kitchen Basics, Pacifica, or Progresso chicken broth

¼ cup cilantro, chopped

¼ cup Italian parsley, chopped

3-4 oz bittersweet chocolate or to taste

2 Tbsp honey or to taste

Queso fresco, goat cheese, or crème fraîche to garnish

Heat oil and butter in a stockpot over medium-high heat until butter melts. Add onion and sauté until translucent, approximately 5 minutes. Add garlic and sauté for 1 minute until fragrant. Add carrots, celery, and sun-dried tomatoes. Season with salt, pepper, harissa, paprika, cumin, and coriander. Sauté for a couple of minute to toast spices and soften vegetables. Add wine and continue cooking on high until all of the liquid has evaporated. Add tomatoes and chicken broth. Bring to a boil. Cover and reduce heat to a simmer. Cook for 45 minutes or until the vegetables are tender. Add parsley, cilantro, chocolate, and honey. Purée completely with an immersion blender. Adjust seasoning, amount of chocolate, and amount of honey to taste. Serve hot, garnished with queso fresco, fresh goat cheese, or homemade crème fraîche.

Relax in the parlo
or on the sun porc

Broccoli Cheese Soup

I don't know about you, but I hate a broccoli cheese soup that has been thickened with flour and is so dense that a spoon can stand straight up in it. I want my soup to be rich and creamy, not like glue. This broccoli cheese soup does just that. By puréeing the soup, you get the consistency of a thickening agent without the flour or cornstarch. Velveeta has no place in this soup. It might melt well, but processed cheeses are not only bad for you, they may contain ingredients that are not appropriate for a gluten-free lifestyle.

Yields Approximately 8 Servings

3 Tbsp extra virgin olive oil

2 Tbsp unsalted butter

1 medium onion, diced

2 carrots, peeled and diced

2 celery sticks, diced

3 large heads of broccoli, trimmed and cut into smaller florets

2-3 garlic cloves, minced

Pinch kosher salt and freshly ground pepper

2 bay leaves

2 tsp Hungarian smoked hot paprika

2 Tbsp herbes de Provence

½ cup dry sherry or dry vermouth

4-6 cups Kitchen Basics, Pacifica, or Progresso chicken broth

½-¾ cup Daisy sour cream

1 cup aged cheddar, grated

In a medium stockpot, heat butter and olive oil over medium-high heat until butter has melted. Add onions and sauté until tender and just barely golden, approximately 5 minutes. Add garlic and cook for 1 minute until fragrant. Add celery and carrots and sauté 5 minutes or until the vegetables begin to soften. Add broccoli and spices. Sauté for a minute or two to toast the spices. Deglaze the pan with vermouth or sherry and turn the heat to high. Cook uncovered until all the liquid has evaporated. Add chicken broth and bring to a boil. Cover and simmer on low heat for 45 minutes. Turn heat off and remove bay leaves. Using an immersion blender, purée soup to a smooth consistency. Add sour cream and cheese. Purée again to combine. Adjust seasonings to taste. Serve hot with a dollop of homemade crème fraîche.

Valentine's Day Dinner

Valentine's Day is always so stressful with trying to figure out what to get a lover or spouse that they don't already have and finding a place to go for a romantic meal where you won't be surrounded by screaming kids and it won't cost you a fortune. Why not consider staying at home and cooking a romantic meal for two? I guarantee it'll be the best gift you could give your significant other and they will thank you for years to come. To set the mood, light plenty of candles, play some soft jazz, and have a nice glass of champagne waiting when they arrive.

Spinach Salad with Pomegranate Seeds, Dried Cranberries, Roasted Pistachios, and Shaved Parmesan Cheese

I know that Valentine's Day isn't exactly the time to think about health, but this salad is a nutritional powerhouse. Spinach is loaded with iron and folic acid, cranberries and pomegranates are super high in antioxidants, and pistachios are abundant in good-for-you unsaturated fats. And of course, they all taste great! Note: Pomegranates can be tricky to work with. They have a natural dye that will stain your entire kitchen if you aren't careful. To easily and cleanly remove the seeds, cut the pomegranate in half and place in a large bowl of water. You can pop the seeds straight into the water. The seeds will sink while the pith and peel float to the top for easy skimming, and the color stays right in the bowl.

YIELDS 2 SERVINGS

2 cups baby spinach leaves

2 Tbsp pomegranate seeds

2 Tbsp dried cranberries

2 oz shaved Parmesan cheese

2 Tbsp roasted pistachios

¼ cup extra virgin olive oil

1 Tbsp sherry

1 Tbsp raspberry balsamic vinaigrette

1 Tbsp Grey Poupon Dijon mustard

1 Tbsp honey

Pinch kosher salt and freshly ground pepper

For dressing, place oil, vinegar, sherry, mustard, honey, salt, and pepper in a tightly sealing Tupperware container. Shake vigorously to combine (but see p. 101). Toss spinach gently with dressing. Place on two plates. Garnish with pomegranate seeds, cranberries, pistachios, and Parmesan.

Seared Scallops with Avocado and North African Mango Chutney

While this recipe yields far more chutney than you need for two people, it freezes really well and can be used as an accompaniment for chicken, pork, or fish for a future meal. So kill two birds with one stone. It's the gift that keeps on giving.

YIELDS 2 SERVINGS WITH EXTRA CHUTNEY

For the chutney
- 2 lbs mango, peeled and chopped
- 2 Tbsp extra virgin olive oil
- ½ tsp harissa
- ½ red onion, diced
- ½ red bell pepper, seeded and diced
- 2 garlic cloves, minced
- Pinch ground ginger
- Pinch saffron
- Pinch kosher salt and freshly ground pepper
- 4 oz orange juice
- 2 oz red wine vinegar
- ¼ cup honey
- ½ tsp orange zest
- 1 tsp orange blossom water
- 2 tsp ras el hanout
- ¼ cup dried cranberries
- ¼ cup toasted pistachios

For the scallops
- 2 sea scallops
- Pinch kosher salt and freshly ground pepper
- Pinch Hungarian hot paprika
- 2 tsp unsalted butter
- ¼ cup dry sherry
- ½ avocado

Heat olive oil in a medium sauté pan over medium-high heat. Add onion and sauté until translucent, approximately 5 minutes. Add harissa and heat through 1 minute. Add garlic and sauté for 1 minute until fragrant. Add bell pepper, ginger, saffron, salt, and pepper and sauté an additional minute until the spices are toasted. Add mango and sauté for a minute just to heat through. Turn off heat. Add orange juice, vinegar, honey, orange zest, orange blossom water, and ras el hanout to the pan. Turn heat back on and bring to a boil. Reduce heat to a simmer and simmer uncovered for approximately 30 minutes or until the liquid has mostly evaporated and the chutney has thickened. Season to taste. Transfer to a bowl over an ice bath. Add cranberries and pistachios and stir to combine. Once cooled, cover with plastic wrap and place in the refrigerator. Let sit at least 4 hours or up to overnight for the flavors to mature.

Pat scallops dry with a paper towel. Season with salt, pepper, and paprika. Heat butter in a medium sauté pan over medium-high heat until the butter begins to brown. Add scallops and sear on one side. Turn over and deglaze the pan with sherry. Continue cooking until the scallops are just cooked through but not rubbery, approximately 5 minutes. To serve, place about a tablespoon of the chutney on a small plate. Cut the avocado into quarters and place one quarter of an avocado over the chutney. Top with seared scallop and serve immediately.

Steak Diane

Steak Diane used to be a very popular dish in restaurants in the 50s and 60s. It sort of disappeared with the introduction of "fusion cuisine" and "molecular gastronomy" in recent years, but it is a classic that is worth reintroducing into your regular repertoire. It is elegant, delicious, and remarkably simple to make.

YIELDS 2 SERVINGS

For the steaks
- 2 ¾-inch filet mignons
- Kosher salt and freshly ground pepper
- 1 tsp garlic powder
- 2 tsp herbes de Provence
- 2 tsp extra virgin olive oil

For the sauce
- 1 Tbsp unsalted butter
- 1 Tbsp extra virgin olive oil
- 1 shallot, sliced
- 2 garlic cloves, minced
- ½ cup sliced button mushrooms
- Kosher salt and freshly ground pepper
- 2 tsp herbes de Provence
- Pinch freshly grated nutmeg
- ¼ cup dry sherry or dry vermouth
- 3 Tbsp heavy cream
- 1 tsp Grey Poupon Dijon mustard
- 2 Tbsp Kitchen Basics, Pacifica, or Progresso beef broth
- 1 tsp Lea & Perrins Worcestershire sauce
- ½ tsp harissa
- 1 scallion, chopped
- 1 tsp Italian parsley, minced

Drizzle 2 tsp olive oil on the filets and season liberally with salt, pepper, garlic powder, and herbes de Provence. Place filets in the refrigerator for at least 3 hours or up to overnight to marinate. Remove from the refrigerator approximately 30 minutes before grilling. Using an indoor grill pan or outdoor grill, grill to medium-rare or medium. Wrap tightly in foil while making the sauce.

For the sauce, heat butter and oil in a medium sauté pan over medium-high heat until the butter has melted. Add shallot slices and sauté for a couple of minutes or until they begin to get golden. Add garlic and sauté for 1 minute until it is fragrant. Add mushrooms and season with salt, pepper, herbes de Provence, and nutmeg. Stir to combine. Deglaze the pan with the sherry or vermouth and continue cooking on high until all the liquid has evaporated and the mushrooms begin to caramelize. Add mustard, cream, broth, Worcestershire, and harissa. Heat through and cook until the sauce is thick and creamy. Add scallion and parsley to sauce at the last minute before serving.

To serve, unwrap filets from foil and pour any juices that have been left behind into the sauce. Garnish with sauce.

Goat Cheese Risotto

Risotto is something that appears difficult to make. In reality it just takes a lot of patience. You can't rush it or the rice will never cook properly. Note: The creaminess of this rice isn't accomplished through the addition of cream, contrary to popular belief. Arborio rice is naturally quite starchy. As it cooks slowly, these starches leach out of the rice, creating a creamy sauce-like quality that is what makes risotto so unique and delicious. To help with timing this dish, you can cook it until it is almost finished and most of the liquid has been added and then turn it off. Add the remaining liquid to the pot and the rice will continue absorbing the liquid slowly, finishing off the cooking process with residual heat while you complete the sauce for the steak. Risotto does not keep. It must be served immediately once it is done or it will become gummy.

YIELDS 2 SERVINGS

1 Tbsp unsalted butter
1 Tbsp extra virgin olive oil
½ onion, diced
2 garlic cloves, minced
½ cup arborio rice
1 tsp herbes de Provence

Kosher salt and freshly ground pepper
⅛ cup dry sherry
2-3 cups chicken broth, heated to a simmer in a small stockpot
2 oz goat cheese

Heat butter and oil in a medium stockpot. Add onion and sauté until translucent, approximately 5 minutes. Add garlic and sauté for 1 minute until fragrant. Add rice and sauté for 1 minute to toast. Season with salt, pepper, and herbes de Provence. Deglaze pan with sherry and continue to cook over medium heat until all the liquid has been absorbed. Reduce heat to medium-low and slowly add 1 ladleful of the stock to the pot at a time, stirring continuously, until the rice is just al dente and creamy, approximately 30-40 minutes. Add cheese and stir in to melt. Adjust seasoning to taste.

Poached Pears in a Port or Marsala and Orange Sauce

Fruit desserts are always a light and delicious finale to an elegant dinner. They satisfy a sweet tooth without being overly rich or filling so you can enjoy the rest of your evening in comfort. Keep the remaining sauce for up to a week in the refrigerator. It is delicious on ice cream or as a substitute for maple syrup in topping pancakes.

YIELDS 2 SERVINGS

2 medium Bosc pears, peeled and cored using a melon baller
1½ cups port or Marsala
1 cup orange juice, preferably with pulp
½ cup granulated sugar
1 tsp ground cinnamon
Pinch ground cloves

Pinch freshly grated nutmeg
½ tsp ground cardamom
½ tsp ground ginger
Pinch freshly ground pepper
1 tsp pure vanilla extract
2 tsp orange blossom water

Place the port, orange juice, sugar, cinnamon, cloves, nutmeg, cardamom, ginger, peppercorns, vanilla, and orange blossom water in a medium saucepan. Heat on medium-high and bring to a boil. Add pears. Bring to a boil again and then reduce to a simmer. Simmer uncovered for approximately 20 minutes or until a knife inserted into the pears comes out cleanly. Bring the sauce to a boil and reduce by half, which should take about an additional 20 minutes. Cool syrup and pears and refrigerate 8 hours or overnight. Serve cold, garnished with whipped cream, Häagen Dazs vanilla ice cream, or mascarpone cream.

Mascarpone Cream

4 oz mascarpone, at room
   temperature
1 Tbsp heavy whipping
   cream

1 tsp vanilla extract
½ tsp ground cinnamon
1-2 Tbsp honey

Beat mascarpone with heavy whipping cream until light and fluffy. Add flavorings and sweeten to taste with the honey.

Fourth of July Party

Whⁿen it comes to the Fourth of July, most of us want to make something easy that will keep well for a few hours. Here are a handful of recipes that are twists on some standard favorites and are good served hot or cold. Add some gluten-free beer and fireworks and you're good to go.

Community fireworks in Bureau County, Illinois

Moroccan Spiced Hot Wings

I'm a wing fiend. While I like the fried ones you can get in a bar like the next guy, they are not only bad for your waistline, but obviously not gluten-free. Here is another exotic twist on an old favorite that takes away some of the fat, all of the gluten, but none of the flavor. It is finger food at its best. Just make sure to provide plenty of wet naps!

YIELDS APPROXIMATELY 8 SERVINGS

2 lbs wings/drumettes
2-3 Tbsp extra virgin
olive oil
2 Tbsp honey
2 Tbsp harissa

Pinch kosher salt and
freshly ground pepper
2 tsp garlic powder
2 tsp Hungarian hot
paprika

Combine wings/drumettes in a large bowl with all the ingredients. Toss well. Cover and refrigerate for at least 2 hours. Place in a single layer on a baking sheet and bake at 375 degrees for approximately 30 minutes or until the chicken is cooked through and begins to caramelize on top.

Creamed Spinach

Another great go-to side dish that is quick and easy. Be sure not to skimp on the nutmeg. I add nutmeg to any green leafy vegetable including kale, collard greens, and swiss chard. It gives the dish a certain je ne sais quoi, or in English, "I don't know what!"

YIELDS 6-8 SERVINGS

2 lbs fresh baby spinach leaves
3 shallots, sliced
2-3 garlic cloves, minced
2 Tbsp unsalted butter
2 Tbsp extra virgin olive oil
Pinch kosher salt and freshly ground pepper

Pinch freshly grated nutmeg
1 Tbsp Domata Living Flour
½ cup heavy cream
½ cup grated Parmesan cheese

Heat butter and oil in a sauté pan over medium-high heat. Add shallots and sauté until softened. Add garlic and sauté 1 minute or until fragrant. Add spinach and season with salt, pepper, and nutmeg. Cook uncovered until the spinach has wilted and all the liquid has evaporated. Add flour and sauté for a couple of minutes to cook the rawness out of the flour. Add cream and bring to a simmer. Add Parmesan and heat through to melt. Adjust seasoning to taste.

Mixed Bean Salad—Palikaria

What family doesn't have a recipe for a three-bean salad? This is a Mediterranean twist on the tradition and wonderful for an outdoor party because it does not have mayonnaise in it and therefore can sit at room temperature for a while without refrigeration. Make it in advance, as the flavors will continue to develop as it sits.

YIELDS APPROXIMATELY 8-10 SERVINGS

1 can red kidney beans, drained
1 can pinto beans, drained
1 can chickpeas, drained
1 cup cooked quinoa
½ cup lentils
½ cup frozen peas

Kosher salt and freshly ground pepper
2 green onions, chopped
2-3 garlic cloves, minced
1 Tbsp fresh dill, minced
½ cup extra virgin olive oil
2 Tbsp lemon juice

Heat 3-4 cups water to a boil in a medium saucepan. Season with salt. Add lentils and peas and cook approximately 15 minutes or until tender. Drain. Place beans, quinoa, lentils, peas, green onions, and garlic in a mixing bowl. Add salt, pepper, dill, olive oil, and lemon juice. Toss to combine. Season to taste. Serve cold or at room temperature.

Carrot and Parsnip Purée

Parsnips are one of those vegetables that most people don't know how to use, which is a huge shame. They are not only tremendously healthy but they are a unique taste and texture that really adds depth to almost any soup or stew. Try them roasted as well. You can peel and chunk them, toss them in olive oil, and season with salt and pepper. Roast until tender and golden, and—voila!

YIELDS **4** SERVINGS

4 carrots, peeled and sliced into 1" chunks
4 parsnips, peeled and sliced into 1" chunks
6-8 garlic cloves, peeled

Kosher salt and freshly ground pepper
1 stick unsalted butter
¼-½ cup grated Parmesan cheese
¼-½ cup heavy cream

Place carrots, parsnips, and garlic in a medium saucepan. Cover with cold water and season liberally with salt. Bring to a boil and cook for approximately 30 minutes or until the carrots and parsnips are tender and cooked through. Drain. Place in a food processor with butter and Parmesan, and season with salt and pepper. Purée, adding enough cream to make the purée smooth. Adjust seasoning to taste.

Coconut Macaroons

My husband, who professes to hate coconut, considers this one of his absolute favorite desserts. They are sweet but light so you don't feel guilty eating one after a heavy meal. They also keep beautifully. Place in an airtight container and keep for up to one week. They are as moist on day seven as they were on day one.

14 oz sweetened coconut
1 can Carnation
  sweetened condensed
  milk
1 tsp vanilla extract

1 tsp ground cinnamon
2 egg whites
Pinch kosher salt
Pinch cream of tartar

Beat egg whites together with salt and cream of tartar until stiff peaks form. In a separate bowl, stir together coconut, milk, vanilla, and cinnamon. Gently fold egg whites into coconut mixture until well combined. Using an ice cream scoop, scoop macaroons onto a baking sheet lined with parchment paper, leaving approximately 2 inches between macaroons. Bake in a preheated 325 degree oven for 30 minutes. Allow to cool completely before serving.

Light Summer Fare

This is a fabulous summer menu for several reasons. First, when it is hot and humid, nobody wants to eat something heavy and hard to digest. Second, most of us are watching our waistlines in the summer months and this menu allows us to eat well without feeling like we can't put on that cute bathing suit. Third, it takes advantage of the bounty of fresh vegetables in the summer. And finally, it is all gluten-free.

The gardens at Chestnut Street Inn

Tomato Bisque Soup

Think of this soup as a great alternative to a Campbell's tomato soup. Much higher in flavor and certainly a lot healthier. It uses honey, which is a natural sweetener, to cut the acidity of the tomatoes, and the addition of a small amount of Parmigiano or Pecorino Romano cheese is a great way to add a kick of flavor without a lot of fat.

YIELDS 6-8 SERVINGS

2-3 Tbsp extra virgin
  olive oil
1 Spanish onion, chopped
2-3 garlic cloves, minced
1 carrot, peeled and diced
2 celery stalks, diced
1 28-oz can ciced
  tomatoes
1 4-oz pkg sun-dried
  tomatoes, sliced
Kosher salt and freshly
  ground pepper

1 bay leaf
2 Tbsp herbes de Provence
¼ cup dry vermouth or
  dry sherry
4-6 cups chicken broth
2 Tbsp honey
½ cup Pecorino Romano
  or Parmigiano
  Reggiano, freshly
  grated, plus some to
  garnish

Heat olive oil in a medium stockpot over medium-high heat. Add onion and sauté until translucent, approximately 5 minutes. Add garlic and sauté for 1 minute until fragrant. Add carrots, celery, and sun-dried tomatoes. Season with salt, pepper, bay leaf, and herbes de Provence. Deglaze the pan with vermouth or sherry and bring to a boil. Reduce on high until all the liquid has evaporated. Add tomatoes and chicken broth and bring to a boil. Cover and reduce heat to a simmer. Cook for approximately 45 minutes. Remove bay leaves and purée soup with an immersion blender until smooth and creamy. Season to taste with salt, pepper, and honey. Add freshly grated Pecorino Romano or Parmigiano Reggiano and purée one last time to incorporate. Serve hot with additional grated cheese if desired.

Zucchini Stuffed with Caramelized Onions, Tomatoes and Cheese — Imam Bayildi

The name of this traditional Turkish dish literally translates to "the Imam fainted." An Imam is a Muslim religious teacher. There are two stories about why he might have fainted. One is that he was so enraptured by the taste of this dish. The other is that he was floored by how expensive the ingredients were. Either way, it is a delicious and healthy first course.

YIELDS 12 SERVINGS

6 medium zucchini, cut in half lengthwise and seeds scooped out with a melon baller
2 onions, sliced
3-4 garlic cloves, minced
Kosher salt and freshly ground pepper
2-3 Tbsp extra virgin olive oil
1 tsp Hungarian smoked hot paprika
1 tsp ground cumin

1 28-oz can diced tomatoes
½ cup Italian parsley, chopped
½ cup cilantro, chopped
2 Tbsp extra virgin olive oil
2 Tbsp sugar
2 tsp kosher salt
½ cup Kitchen Basics, Pacifica, or Progresso chicken broth
8 oz feta, crumbled (Don't buy pre-crumbled feta. Do it yourself.)

Heat olive oil in a medium sauté pan over medium-high heat. Add onions and sauté until onions begin to caramelize, approximately 8 minutes. Add garlic and sauté for 1 minute or until fragrant. Add tomatoes, salt, pepper, cumin, paprika, parsley, and butcher cilantro. Reduce heat and simmer uncovered until almost all the liquid has evaporated and the flavors are concentrated. Season to taste and cool. Place zucchini halves on a shallow baking dish and season with salt, sugar, and a drizzle of olive oil. Distribute filling amongst zucchini halves. Top with feta. Add chicken broth to the baking sheet and place in a 350 degree oven for approximately 25-30 minutes or until the zucchini are tender and cooked through. Remove from oven and allow to sit for approximately 10 minutes before serving.

Ratatouille

While this was the name of a very cute animated flick, it is also the name of a marvelous classic French side dish. Loaded with vegetables, this dish is one that every household in France has its own recipe for. Mine happens to have a slight Moroccan influence to it with the addition of cilantro and harissa. Leftovers of this are great, as the flavors will simply continue to develop in the refrigerator. Eat cold like a salad or reheat it as a side dish.

YIELDS 8 SERVINGS

1 medium globe eggplant, sliced ¼" thick
2 zucchini, sliced ¼" thick
2 yellow squash, sliced ¼" thick
1 large Spanish onion, sliced
2-3 garlic cloves, minced
2-3 Tbsp extra virgin olive oil, plus more for frying
1 28-oz can diced tomatoes

2 red bell peppers, roasted (see p. 53), peeled, seeded, and cut into slices
3 Tbsp Italian parsley, minced
3 Tbsp cilantro, minced
Kosher salt and freshly ground pepper
1 Tbsp harissa or pinch of cayenne pepper
½ cup freshly grated Parmesan or Pecorino Romano

Place eggplant and squash slices on paper towels and salt liberally. Cover with another layer of paper towels and allow to sit for 30 minutes to an hour to remove moisture from the vegetables. Fry vegetables in shallow olive oil until crispy. Place on paper towels to drain. Season with pepper. Heat 2-3 tablespoons olive oil in a medium skillet over medium-high heat. Add onions and sauté for approximately 8 minutes or until softened and lightly caramelized. Add garlic and sauté for 1 minute or until fragrant. Add tomatoes. Season with salt and pepper. Reduce heat to medium and sauté until most of the liquid has evaporated, approximately 30 minutes. Add parsley, cilantro, and harissa or cayenne. Adjust seasoning to taste. In a 9" x 13" Pyrex baking dish, alternate layers of the eggplant and squash chips with roasted pepper slices and tomato mixture, making two layers of each. Top the vegetables with freshly grated cheese and place in a 350 degree oven for approximately 15 minutes or until the cheese is melted and begins to brown slightly. Let cool for 10 minutes before serving.

Fish en Papillote with Julienne Vegetables (Fish in Parchment Paper)

"En Papillote" literally translates to "in paper." Baking fish in parchment paper creates steam within the packets, keeping it moist and delicious without adding a lot of fat. Salmon is well known for its health benefits. It is super high in omega 3 fatty acids and a great source of unsaturated fats, as are the olives.

YIELDS 4 SERVINGS

4-6 oz salmon filets
2-3 Tbsp extra virgin olive oil
½ cup pitted Kalamata olives
2 Tbsp capers
1 lemon, sliced

Kosher salt and freshly ground pepper
2 Roma tomatoes, sliced
2-3 Tbsp Italian parsley, chopped
¼ cup lemon juice

Preheat oven to 350 degrees.

Cut 4 squares of parchment paper, approximately 8" x 8". Place each salmon filet in the center of a paper square. Season fish with salt and pepper. Drizzle with olive oil. Distribute olives, capers, lemon slices, tomato slices, and parsley evenly amongst fish packets. Drizzle each with some of the lemon juice. Fold parchment in half and seal by crimping edges all the way around and tucking the final edge underneath. If the seal won't hold, you can staple it shut, just remember to remove the staples prior to serving. Bake for approximately 25 minutes or until the parchment packets are puffed. Remove and cut a hole in each packet with a knife, folding back the parchment to serve.

Macerated Strawberries with Balsamic Reduction and Mascarpone Cream

This is a very traditional Italian dessert. Macerating simply refers to the process of allowing the strawberries to marinate in their own juices, which have been drawn out by the addition of the sugar. The use of vinegar may sound odd, but once the vinegar is reduced, the acidity is removed and what is left behind is a sweet, syrupy sauce that is a marvelous contrast with the sweetness of the strawberries.

YIELDS 8 SERVINGS

2 pints fresh strawberries
2-3 Tbsp sugar

3-4 Tbsp balsamic reduction (see p. 38)
8 Tbsp mascarpone cream (see p. 140)

Cut off ends of strawberries and halve berries. Sprinkle with sugar and toss to coat evenly. Allow strawberries to sit for at least 30 minutes before serving. Distribute evenly amongst 8 bowls. Drizzle with balsamic reduction and top with a dollop of the mascarpone cream.

Holiday Party

I don't know about you, but I get a little bored with the same old dry turkey and ham at Thanksgiving and Christmas. And as far as I'm concerned, most of the traditional fare served during the holidays is an absolute carbo load that puts everyone into a coma and makes us all feel bloated. With that in mind, nobody will miss the heavy faves which are obviously not gluten-free, and everyone will thank you for an elegant, delicious holiday meal the whole family can enjoy.

Pumpkin Soup

Pumpkins aren't just for carving. They are delicious, healthy, and a seasonal vegetable in the fall that is a great addition to any meal. I have experimented with using fresh pie pumpkins that I have baked in this dish and decided that the extra effort really wasn't worth it. The canned pumpkin is really perfectly suited for a soup and the flavor very comparable to the fresh

YIELD: APPROXIMATELY 8 SERVINGS

2 14-oz cans pumpkin (Be sure not to use pumpkin pie filling.)
2 medium onions, chopped
2 medium carrots, peeled and chopped
2 celery stalks, chopped
2 garlic cloves, minced
2 Tbsp extra virgin olive oil
2 Tbsp unsalted butter
3 tsp kosher salt

1 tsp freshly ground pepper
Pinch freshly grated nutmeg
2 tsp Hungarian smoked hot paprika
2 bay leaves
2 Tbsp herbes de Provence
½ cup vermouth or dry sherry
6 cups chicken stock
½-¾ cup sour cream
2-3 Tbsp honey

Heat olive oil and butter in a medium soup pot over med-high heat. Once the butter has melted, add onions and sauté until tender, approximately 5 minutes. Add garlic and sauté 1 minute until fragrant. Add carrots, celery, and remaining spices and sauté for a couple of minutes to toast the spices. Add the pumpkin and then deglaze the pan with the ½ cup vermouth or sherry. Bring heat to high and reduce the liquid until most of it has evaporated. Add chicken stock and bring to a boil. Cover and reduce heat to a simmer. Simmer covered for 45 minutes. Turn off heat and remove bay leaves. Using an immersion blender, purée the soup until creamy. Add sour cream and honey and purée until the sour cream is well incorporated. Adjust seasoning to taste. Serve hot with a dollop of crème fraîche.

Maple-Glazed Pork Loin

To me maple conjures up the smells of the holidays. It is a natural sweetener, and the sugars in the maple will caramelize on the pork, giving it a beautiful golden color. If you can find it, use pastured pork, which is free range and grass fed. Commercially produced pork has been genetically modified to breed out most of its natural fat, which has left us with pork that is virtually fat free, ergo, flavor free. It also ends up incredibly dry. Also, keep in mind, pork is no longer considered to be a health risk and should not be cooked to the point of incineration. Trichinosis, the one potential hazardous bacteria in pork, is destroyed at 130 degrees. You should cook pork to medium-rare or medium with a good hint of pink, not unlike a steak. This will ensure it remains juicy, and you will taste its full flavor. You are aiming for approximately 140 degrees when you remove it from the oven, and then there will still be some carry-over cooking time that will raise it an additional 10 degrees or so.

YIELDS APPROXIMATELY 8-10 SERVINGS

3-4 lb boneless pork loin
Pinch kosher salt and
   freshly ground pepper
1 tsp ground ginger
1 tsp Hungarian smoked
   hot paprika
1 tsp garlic powder
1 tsp herbes de Provence

Pam cooking spray
2 Tbsp extra virgin olive
   oil
¼ cup pure maple syrup
¼ cup sugar
3 Tbsp La Choy soy sauce
1 Tbsp Grey Poupon
   Dijon mustard

Drizzle pork loin with 2 Tbsp olive oil. Season the pork loin liberally on all sides with salt, pepper, ginger, paprika, garlic powder, and herbes de Provence. Place the pork loin in the refrigerator for approximately 3 hours to marinate. Remove roast from the refrigerator at least ½ hour prior to roasting. Prepare the basting sauce by combining syrup, sugar, soy sauce, mustard, and a pinch of pepper. Preheat oven to 350 degrees. Place the pork loin in the oven and roast for approximately one hour or until the internal temperature is 140 degrees, basting with the basting sauce approximately 3 times during the roasting process. Remove from the oven and cover tightly with aluminum foil. Allow roast to rest for at least 20 minutes to allow the juices to redistribute themselves before cutting into the roast.

Whipped Sweet Potatoes

Forget your sweet potatoes with marshmallows. This is a savory side dish worthy of any elegant dinner. Note that I say start in cold water. This is a key with both sweet potatoes and regular potatoes when cooking to mash. If you cover them with hot water, it will draw the natural starch out of the potatoes and make them gummy.

YIELDS APPROXIMATELY 8 SERVINGS

4 large sweet potatoes, peeled and cubed into 1" pieces
Pinch kosher salt and freshly ground pepper
1 stick unsalted butter
1-2 tablespoons honey or pure maple syrup
¼-½ cup heavy cream
¼-½ cup grated Parmesan cheese
1 head roasted garlic (see p. 104)

Place sweet potato pieces in a pot and cover with cold water. Season with a good pinch of salt and place on a burner over high heat. Bring to a boil and allow to simmer uncovered for approximately 30 minutes or until the potatoes are tender. Remove from heat and drain. Season the potatoes with salt, pepper, and honey. Add butter, cream, Parmesan cheese, and all of the roasted garlic. Mash until smooth and creamy, adjusting amounts of salt, pepper, honey, and Parmesan to taste. Don't place in a food processor or the sweet potatoes will become gummy.

Creamed Corn

Affectionately named "Jesus Corn" by a cooking-class student of mine, this is one of my most popular side dishes. When we made them in class, she said eating it was like a religious experience—hence the title. You judge for yourself.

YIELDS APPROXIMATELY 8 SERVINGS

6 slices bacon, chopped
3 leeks or 1 large onion,
  chopped
2-3 garlic cloves, minced
6 ears fresh sweet corn,
  cut off the cob

Pinch kosher salt and
  freshly ground pepper
2 Tsps herbes de Provence
2-3 Tbsp Domata Living
  Flour
2-3 Tbsp honey
½ cup heavy cream

Sauté bacon in a medium sauté pan over medium-high heat until crisp. Add onion or leek and cook until translucent, approximately 5 minutes. Add garlic and cook for 1 minute until fragrant. Add corn and season with salt, pepper, and herbes de Provence. Add flour and honey and sauté to toast flour, approximately 1 minute. Add cream and continue to cook until thick and creamy. Adjust seasoning to taste.

Sweet Potato Pots de Crème

Literally translated, pots de crème means "pots of cream" and is traditionally made with canned pumpkin. I decided to try sweet potato as a substitute to see if I could recreate the idea of a sweet potato pie, since I'm not really a pie fan and of course pie crust isn't gluten-free. It was a huge hit.

YIELDS 6 SERVINGS

1 cup heavy cream
¾ cup whole milk
¾ cup pure maple syrup
½ cup cooked and mashed
   sweet potato
7 egg yolks
1 tsp ground cinnamon

Pinch ground cloves
Pinch freshly grated
   nutmeg
Pinch ground ginger
1 tsp pure vanilla extract
Pinch kosher salt

Preheat oven to 325 degrees. Whisk together cream, milk, syrup, and sweet potato in a small saucepan. Place over medium heat and bring to a simmer. In a separate bowl, whisk together yolks, cinnamon, cloves, nutmeg, ginger, vanilla, and salt until pale and creamy. Slowly whisk in cream mixture a little at a time, whisking constantly to temper egg yolks. Pour custard through a strainer into a large Pyrex measuring cup. Place six 1-cup ramekins in a large Pyrex baking dish. Distribute custard mix evenly amongst the ramekins and pour hot water approximately ¼ the way up the baking dish, creating a hot water bath. Bake for approximately 35-40 minutes or until the custard is just set, like Jell-O. Remove custards from the oven and allow to cool for 1 hour. Cover each with plastic wrap and place in the refrigerator. Allow to chill for at least 2 hours before serving. Can be made in advance and kept in the refrigerator for up to one week. Serve with a dollop of homemade whipped cream or a small scoop of Häagen Dazs vanilla ice cream.

Brunch

Who doesn't love a weekend brunch? As a bed and breakfast we of course specialize in breakfast, but brunch is also a fabulous way to entertain. Something different where you can have a party and still have the rest of the day ahead of you.

Dried Cranberry Scones

What tea party is complete without a scone? Unfortunately what most of us think of as scones are pretty dense hockey pucks that are generally found at the popular chain of coffee shops which shall remain nameless. These are light and flaky and are delicious dunked in a cup of hot Earl Grey tea with milk.

YIELDS 8 SERVINGS

2 cups Domata Living Flour
2 Tbsp granulated sugar
Pinch kosher salt
½ tsp baking soda
2 tsp baking powder

1 stick of unsalted butter, cubed
½ cup dried cranberries
1 cup buttermilk (see p. 164)
1 egg, separated

Combine flour, sugar, baking soda, baking powder, and salt. Using a pastry cutter, cut butter in until the mixture has pea-size granules in it. Add dried cranberries and toss to coat. Add egg yolk to buttermilk and pour into dry mixture. Using a fork, combine until most of moisture has been absorbed. Continue kneading until just combined but do not over-knead. Transfer to an ungreased baking sheet and flatten into a disc about ½ inch thick. Using a pizza wheel, cut into 8 pieces. Brush with egg white and sprinkle with approximately 1 Tbsp sugar. Place into a preheated 375 degree oven for approximately 20 minutes or until golden brown.

Corn Hotcakes

These hotcakes look substantial, like a pancake, but are light and fluffy. The buttermilk reacts with the baking powder/soda to create pockets of air that make them puff up. Note: These will turn out better if you allow the batter to sit for 30 minutes before cooking up the hotcakes.

A quick substitution note. If you don't have buttermilk, don't fret. You can use whole milk combined with lemon juice or white wine vinegar. The rule of thumb is that for every 1 cup of milk use 1 Tbsp lemon juice or vinegar and allow to stand for 10 minutes.

Yields Approximately 12 cakes

1 cup Domata Living
  Flour
¼ cup granulated sugar
¾ cup yellow cornmeal
¼ tsp kosher salt
½ tsp baking soda
3½ tsp baking powder
1 tsp ground cinnamon
Pinch ground cloves
Pinch freshly grated
  nutmeg
½ tsp cardamom

1 tsp ground ginger
1½ cups buttermilk
3 Tbsp melted unsalted
  butter
2 eggs
1 tsp pure vanilla extract
½ cup raspberries,
  blueberries, or
  quartered strawberries
Additional butter for
  cooking

In a medium mixing bowl, combine flour, sugar, cornmeal, salt, baking soda, baking powder, cloves, nutmeg, cardamom, ginger, and cinnamon. In a separate measuring cup, add melted butter, eggs, and vanilla to the buttermilk and whisk together. Add liquid ingredients to the dry ingredients and stir well to combine. Add fruit and fold into mixture. Using a large skillet or sauté pan over medium heat, place approximately 1 Tbsp butter in the middle of the pan and swirl around to coat pan evenly. Wait until the butter is hot and bubbling. Measure out batter in ¼ measuring cupfuls, spacing them approximately 2 inches apart so they don't run together. Cook on first side until the batter rises a bit and begins to bubble, approximately 5 minutes. Flip the pancake and cook on the other side an additional 3-5 minutes or until golden brown. Continue until all the batter has been used up. Serve hot with maple syrup and butter.

Broccoli, Sun-dried Tomato and Goat Cheese Frittata

A frittata is basically a crustless quiche. In Spain they call them tortas or tortillas. They can be made with practically any vegetable. The key is to use good quality farm fresh eggs if you can get them. The difference is notable. Not only do they have vibrant yellow yolks, but they are firm and flavorful. And if you are eating legitimately cage-free eggs, they are actually lower in cholesterol and saturated fat. Better flavor and better health. That's a win-win situation.

YIELDS APPROXIMATELY 8 SERVINGS

2 Tbsp extra virgin olive oil
2 Tbsp unsalted butter
1 onion, finely chopped
4 garlic cloves, minced
2 broccoli crowns, trimmed and cut into small pieces
¼ cup dry vermouth or dry sherry
3 ounces of fresh goat cheese, crumbled

½ cup chopped sun-dried tomatoes (I prefer the ones jarred in oil over the dried ones)
½ tsp kosher salt
¼ tsp freshly ground pepper
1 tsp Hungarian smoked hot paprika
2 tsp herbes de Provence or Italian seasoning
6 eggs, beaten
½ cup whole milk

Place olive oil and butter in a 10" skillet over medium heat. Once the butter has melted, add onion and cook until it begins to caramelize, approximately 6 minutes. Add garlic and cook for 1 minute or until fragrant. Add broccoli and season with pinch of salt, pepper, paprika, and herbes de Provence. Add vermouth or sherry and cook broccoli until most of the liquid has evaporated. Add sun-dried tomatoes and sauté for a couple of minutes or until the tomatoes begin to rehydrate. In a separate bowl, combine eggs with milk, pinch of salt, and pinch of pepper and beat until well combined. Pour eggs over the broccoli and sun-dried tomatoes. Stir well to combine. Sprinkle the top with the crumbled goat cheese and place in a preheated 375 degree oven for approximately 10-15 minutes or until the eggs have set and the top of the frittata begins to brown slightly. Remove from the oven and let stand for 5 minutes before serving.

Yogurt Parfaits with Orange Blossom Water, Honey, Cinnamon, and Vanilla

Most fruit-filled or flavored yogurts are loaded with sugar and artificial flavorings that none of us need, especially those with gluten intolerances. But flavoring your own is easy, quick, and will taste infinitely better. Be sure to use only gluten-free granolas in this. While oats themselves aren't an issue, remember, they are often processed with the same machines as wheat and therefore can be cross-contaminated.

YIELDS 6-8 SERVINGS

16 oz plain Fage yogurt
2 tsp pure vanilla extract
1 tsp ground cinnamon
2 Tbsp orange blossom
    water

$1/3$-$1/2$ cup orange blossom
    honey
2 cups gluten-free granola
    (Trader Joe's or Enjoy
    Life brand)
2 cups assorted berries

Combine yogurt, cinnamon, orange blossom water, vanilla, and honey and sweeten to taste. Layer yogurt, organic granola, and fresh fruit in a wine glasses. Chill 30 minutes before serving.

Individual Egg and Cheese Souffles

Souffles always seem like such a daunting task. They are actually quite easy to make as long as you follow a couple of simple procedures. First, make sure you beat your egg whites in a metal bowl. If you use glass they have a tendency to slide down the glass and not become light and fluffy. Also, be sure you do not open the oven to peek at the soufflés. Give them the full 20 minutes before looking, and if they aren't golden yet, leave them in for an additional couple of minutes. If you let the hot air escape, they will deflate immediately. Lastly, this isn't a dish you can prepare in advance. You have to make it last minute. My motto is, make the guests wait for the soufflé, not the soufflé wait for the guests.

YIELDS APPROXIMATELY 6 INDIVIDUAL SOUFFLÉS

2 Tbsp unsalted butter
½ cup grated Parmesan cheese
3 Tbsp unsalted butter
3 Tbsp Domata Living Flour
1 cup hot whole milk
1 tsp Grey Poupon Dijon mustard
½ tsp Lea & Perrins Worcestershire sauce
½ tsp harissa
Pinch kosher salt
Pinch freshly grated nutmeg
5 large eggs, separated
Pinch cream of tartar
⅓ cup fresh goat cheese
⅓ cup shredded baby Swiss

Preheat oven to 400 degrees.

Butter 6 1-cup ramekins and place on a baking sheet. Coat each ramekin with Parmesan cheese, tapping the bottom of the ramekins to remove any loose cheese. In a medium saucepan over medium heat, melt butter. Add flour and whisk for approximately 1 minute or until the rawness of the flour begins to cook away. Slowly whisk in hot milk until well combined with the flour and butter mix.

Reduce to low heat and add mustard, Worcestershire sauce, harissa, and nutmeg. Cook on low heat for approximately 5 minutes or until the mixture is thick and creamy. Remove from heat.

Slowly whisk four egg yolks one at a time into base, making sure not to scramble the eggs. Add the swiss and goat cheese and whisk until the cheese is mostly melted. In a separate bowl, beat egg whites with a pinch of cream of tartar and salt until the egg whites form stiff peaks. Take a quarter of the egg whites and whisk them into the yolk/cheese mixture to lighten it. Slowly pour yolk/cheese mixture down the side of the bowl of egg whites and fold remaining whites into the yolk/cheese mixture until well combined. Carefully spoon soufflé mix into individual ramekins, dividing the entire batch evenly amongst the ramekins. Sprinkle the tops of the soufflés with more grated Parmesan cheese.

Place soufflés in the oven and reduce temperature to 375 degrees. Bake for 20 minutes or until the soufflés are puffed and golden on top. Serve immediately.

Roasted Asparagus with Hollandaise Sauce

Hollandaise sauce used to make me sweat until I found Julia Child's recipe. Hers is the only one that doesn't seize up on you and get clumpy within minutes. A simple and effective recipe that works like a charm every time.

YIELDS APPROXIMATELY 8 SERVINGS

For the asparagus
1 lb asparagus
Extra virgin olive oil

Pinch kosher salt and
freshly ground pepper

Preheat oven to 350 degrees. Wash the asparagus and trim the ends off. To determine where to trim the asparagus, take one piece of the asparagus and snap the end off. Trim the remaining asparagus at approximately the same spot as where the piece of asparagus snapped off. Place on a baking sheet. Drizzle generously with olive oil and sprinkle with salt and pepper. Place in the oven and bake approximately 15-18 minutes or until the asparagus is tender and begins to caramelize. Thinner asparagus will take less time than thicker asparagus. For thicker asparagus, use a vegetable peeler to peel off some of the hard stem from the end of the asparagus, revealing only the tender interior. This will enable them to roast faster.

For the hollandaise
3 egg yolks
1 Tbsp water
Pinch kosher salt and
freshly ground pepper

Pinch freshly grated
nutmeg
1 Tbsp lemon juice
1 stick unsalted butter

Place yolks, water, salt, pepper, nutmeg and lemon juice in a small bowl. Using an immersion blender, blend until the yolks are lighter in color and thickened. Melt butter in a small saucepan. Slowly add hot melted butter to yolk mixture, while blending constantly until completely incorporated and thickened. Sauce will hold for up to 2 hours in the refrigerator.

Drizzle sauce over roasted asparagus and serve.

Comfort
Foods

W hen we think of comfort foods, we want things that will provide, well, comfort. Often these are the kind of bad-for-you dishes that are loaded with fat and endorphin-producing sugars and carbs that make you feel warm and fuzzy. Things like fried chicken and dumplings, apple pie, and macaroni and cheese often come to mind. Obviously these pose a problem for those living gluten-free. Fear not, here are some comforting foods that will give you that warm fuzzy feeling and are completely gluten-free.

Iceberg Wedge with Green Goddess Dressing

Mayo is one of those ingredients that just screams comfort to me. It's full of fat, creamy, and delicious. This dressing has plenty of it and is visually stunning with its bright green color. And we all know that avocadoes are a nutritional powerhouse, so you'll feel a little less guilty piling in the full fat mayo. No skimping. If you are going to use it, forget the fat-free or low-fat stuff. The flavor and texture are just not the same.

YIELDS APPROXIMATELY 6 SERVINGS

1 head iceberg lettuce, cut into 6 equal wedges
2 ripe avocadoes
¼ cup Italian parsley
¼ cup basil
¼ cup chives or chopped scallions
2-3 garlic cloves
4 Tbsp fresh lemon juice
2 Tbsp Grey Poupon Dijon mustard

Pinch kosher salt and freshly ground pepper
4 Tbsp Hellmanns mayonnaise
2-3 Tbsp Daisy sour cream
2-3 Tbsp buttermilk (see p. 162)
¼ cup extra virgin olive oil
1 pint of grape tomatoes

Place the avocadoes, parsley, basil, chives, lemon juice, Dijon mustard, salt, pepper, mayonnaise, sour cream, buttermilk, and olive oil in a food processor and purée until smooth. Adjust seasoning to taste. Serve over iceberg wedge with a handful of grape tomatoes.

Crispy Pancetta, Smoked Gouda and Gruyère Mac & Cheese

Who didn't grow up eating mac 'n' cheese? It is the one universally loved food that seems to make everyone happy. Bubbly, oozy, goozy cheese and pasta, it's filling and delicious. But I'm not fond of the stuff that comes in a blue box, so I took it upon myself to take this common childhood *favorite and grow it up a bit with sophisticated flavors like pancetta and cheeses like smoked Gouda and Gruyère. Whatever you do, do not use Velveeta for this. While Velveeta may melt well, it's not cheese. It a processed aberration of a thing posing as cheese. But I digress. Enjoy a trip down memory lane with this dish.*

YIELDS APPROXIMATELY 8 SERVINGS

1 lb gluten-free corn and rice macaroni, cooked "al dente," which literally translates to "to the tooth"

2-3 Tbsp extra virgin olive oil

8 oz pancetta, chopped

2-3 garlic cloves, minced

1 lb sliced button mushrooms

Kosher salt and freshly ground pepper

Pinch freshly grated nutmeg

2 tsp herbes de Provence

½ cup dry vermouth or dry sherry

2 Tbsp Domata Living Flour

1 cup whole milk

1 cup smoked Gouda, grated

1 cup Gruyère, grated

2 Tbsp unsalted butter

Preheat oven to 375 degrees.

Heat olive oil in a medium sauté pan over medium-high heat. Add pancetta and sauté until just lightly crispy and the fat has been rendered. Add garlic and sauté for 1 minute until fragrant. Add mushrooms and season with salt, pepper, nutmeg, and herbes de Provence. Add dry vermouth or dry sherry and sauté on high until all the liquid has evaporated and the mushrooms begin to caramelize. Add flour and sauté for 1 minute to toast the flour. Add the milk and heat through. Adjust seasoning to taste. Add half of each cheese to the mushrooms. Toss with the macaroni and place in a 9" x 11" Pyrex baking dish that has been greased with butter. Cover with remaining cheese and place in the oven for 10-15 minutes or until the cheese is melted and golden. Remove from the oven and allow to sit for 10 minutes before serving.

Irish Stew

A traditional dish around St. Patrick's Day, this is really just a good hearty beef stew that is slow cooking, easy, and will fill your house with wonderful aromas. If you have a good relationship with your butcher, ask him for filet tips. You get the wonderful flavor and texture of a filet without the expense. The final texture of the beef will be so tender it ends up almost like pulled pork.

YIELDS APPROXIMATELY 8-10 SERVINGS

2 ½ lbs beef stew meat
2 Tbsp extra virgin olive oil
1 large onion, diced
2-3 garlic cloves, minced
1 lb baby carrots
1 lb frozen pearl onions, thawed

2 lbs baby red potatoes or Dutch potatoes, washed
4 cups beef broth
Pinch kosher salt and freshly ground pepper
2 bay leaves
2 Tbsp herbes de Provence
3-4 Tbsp Domata Living Flour

Place olive oil in a large stockpot over medium-high heat. Add beef and cook for approximately 5 minutes to brown. Add onion and sauté for 5 minutes until translucent. Add garlic and sauté for 1 minute until fragrant. Add carrots, onions, and potatoes and season with salt, pepper, bay leaves, and herbes de Provence. Add flour and stir for approximately 1 minute to cook through. Add broth and bring to a boil. Cover and reduce to a simmer. Cook for approximately 2 hours, stirring occasionally and adding more liquid if needed. Adjust seasoning to taste. Serve with Daisy sour cream.

Caramelized Maple and Bacon Brussels Sprouts

I know what you're thinking. Brussels sprouts? I hate Brussels sprouts. Well, let me tell you something: so did I until I made this dish. First of all, bacon is a magical food. You could put it on a shoe and it would taste great. Second, the sugar in the maple syrup caramelizes the Brussels sprouts, giving them an intense nutty flavor unlike anything you have ever eaten.

YIELDS 6-8 SERVINGS

1 red onion or 2 shallots, sliced
3-4 garlic cloves, minced
4 slices bacon, chopped
1 lb Brussels sprouts, outer leaves peeled off and hard stems cut back

½ cup dry vermouth or dry sherry
Kosher salt and freshly ground pepper
¼ cup pure maple syrup

Heat medium sauté pan over medium-high heat. Add bacon and sauté until fat is rendered but not crispy. Add onion or shallot and sauté until translucent, approximately 5 minutes. Add garlic and sauté for 1 minute or until fragrant. Add Brussels sprouts and season with salt and pepper. Deglaze the pan with vermouth or sherry and bring to a boil. Cover and reduce to a simmer. Saute for approximately 15 minutes or until the sprouts begin to get tender. Remove lid and turn heat to high. Add maple syrup and reduce until all the liquid has evaporated and the sprouts begin to caramelize. Adjust seasoning to taste.

Flourless Chocolate Cake with Fresh Raspberries and Raspberry Sauce

Chocolate cake is a definite comfort food. But the stuff out of a box is not only not gluten-free, it's just not good. Sorry, Betty Crocker. This is an easy and elegant alternative that will satisfy your sweet tooth and look dynamo when you serve it.

YIELDS APPROXIMATELY 8 SERVINGS

4 oz bittersweet chocolate
1 stick unsalted butter
1 tsp instant coffee granules or 1 Tbsp brewed coffee
1 tsp pure vanilla extract
1 Tbsp ChocoVine
¾ cup granulated sugar
3 large eggs

½ cup unsweetened cocoa powder
2 Tbsp unsalted butter, softened
½ cup seedless raspberry preserves
1 Tbsp water
1 pint fresh raspberries

Preheat oven to 375 degrees.

Grease a 9" springform pan with 2 Tbsp softened butter. Bring a small saucepan of water to a boil. Place bittersweet chocolate, butter, coffee granules, ChocoVine, and vanilla in a heat-proof bowl. Place bowl over saucepan to create a double boiler. Reduce heat to a simmer and whisk chocolate mixture until all the chocolate and butter have melted and the mixture is smooth. Remove from heat. Add sugar, eggs, and sifted cocoa powder. Whisk together until completely smooth. Place in prepared springform pan and bake for approximately 25 minutes. Cool completely. For the raspberry sauce, place preserves and water in a small saucepan. Bring to a boil over high heat and reduce to a simmer. Whisk uncovered until the preserves have melted and the syrup is slightly thickened, approximately 5 minutes. To serve, slice cake into 8 equal wedges. Drizzle each wedge with raspberry sauce and garnish with fresh raspberries.

Dessert Party

An afternoon gathering of just coffee and dessert is another great, informal way of entertaining. I often serve these particular desserts to people with gluten intolerances, who assume they aren't gluten-free. It always comes as a great surprise to them that they are perfectly safe and in fact didn't require much adjustment at all to be gluten-free.

A quick note about coffee, as we always get numerous comments about how great our coffee is here at the inn. Quality beans are one thing, but there are a number of other factors to consider. Coffee loses 80% of its flavor within 15 minutes of grinding. You should always buy whole beans and grind fresh for each pot. Coffee should be stored in a cool, dry place in an airtight container and never in the freezer. Freezing coffee beans will actually break down the cellular structure of the beans, thereby destroying their flavor. Finally, make sure you use good quality filtered water and not tap water. This will eliminate a lot of impurities in the coffee and give it a cleaner, more robust flavor.

Mexican Style Chocolate Mousse

Chocolate mousse is a classic French recipe. This is a twist on the classic that invokes the flavors commonly associated with Mexican hot chocolate, namely chocolate and chili peppers. The heat is subtle, but it creeps up in the back of your throat as you swallow. It is a wonderful little surprise that will catch your guests completely off guard.

Yields Approximately 8-10 Servings

4 eggs, separated
¼ cup brewed coffee
¾ cup granluated sugar
¼ cup ChocoVine (Cabernet Sauvignon blended with fine Dutch chocolate. www.ChocoVine.com. Available through most fine wine purveyors.)

6 oz semi-sweet chocolate
1 tsp pure vanilla extract
1 tsp ground cinnamon
Pinch cayenne pepper
Pinch freshly grated nutmeg
1 stick unsalted butter, softened
Pinch cream of tartar
Pinch kosher salt

Beat yolks, vanilla, cinnamon, pepper, and nutmeg vigorously for a minute or until thick and pale. Place coffee and sugar in a small saucepan over medium heat to melt sugar. Beat melted sugar/coffee mixture slowly into egg yolks to temper. Place ChocoVine and chocolate in a heat-resistant bowl over a saucepan of simmering water. Melt chocolate. Place egg yolks over simmering water and whisk vigorously until thick and pale like Greek yogurt, approximately 5-8 minutes. Remove from heat and beat with hand mixer until double in volume and cooled, approximately 5 minutes. (I actually set the timer on this so that I don't take any shortcuts. Adequate beating is crucial to get the right texture of the mousse.) Add butter to melted chocolate and whisk until smooth. Fold chocolate into yolk mixture. Beat egg whites with cream of tartar and salt until stiff peaks form. Add ¼ of the beaten whites to yolk/chocolate mixture. Fold to lighten. Add remaining whites to yolk/chocolate mixture and fold gently to combine. Place in serving dish or transfer into individual wine glasses for serving. Refrigerate for at least 2-3 hours before serving. Serve with homemade whipping cream and a pinch of cayenne pepper as a garnish.

Amaretto Brownies

These brownies are a moist, fudgy brownie with little flour in the recipe to begin with, so they work great with gluten-free flours. They will keep in an airtight container for up to a week.

YIELDS 9 SMALL BROWNIES

2 oz bittersweet chocolate
1 stick unsalted butter
1 tsp pure vanilla extract
1 tsp granulated instant coffee or 1 Tbsp brewed coffee

1 Tbsp ChocoVine
1 cup granulated sugar
2 eggs
¾ cup Domata Living Flour

Preheat oven to 350 degrees.

Place the chocolate, butter, vanilla, coffee and ChocoVine in a small saucepan over medium-high heat. Whisk until the chocolate and the butter are melted. Remove from heat and allow to cool for about 5 minutes. Whisk in sugar and the eggs one at a time so as not to scramble them. Finally, whisk in the ¾ cup flour and combine until a smooth batter forms. Pour the batter in a greased 8" x 8" x 2" Pyrex baking dish. Bake for 30 minutes. Remove and let cool completely before cutting and serving.

Chocolate Soufflés

Another classic French dessert that appears to be more difficult than it really is. Same rule applies as with all soufflés. Don't peek at the soufflés in the oven or you'll let the heat escape and they'll deflate. Note: If you do not have cream of tartar, which is used to help make egg whites light and fluffy, you can use a tsp of lemon juice. It will have the same effect. Additionally, to guarantee that your egg whites are light and fluffy, always beat them in a metal bowl at room temperature. If you use glass, they will slide down the glass.

YIELDS 4 INDIVIDUAL SOUFFLÉS

1 Tbsp unsalted butter	1 Tbsp brewed coffee or 1
2 tsp sugar	tsp instant coffee
5 oz semi-sweet chocolate	1 Tbsp ChocoVine
chips	2 egg yolks
1 Tbsp unsalted butter	3 egg whites
½ tsp pure vanilla extract	Pinch cream of tartar
	Pinch kosher salt

Preheat oven to 400 degrees.

Coat 4 1-cup glass ramekins with butter and line with granulated sugar, removing any excess by gently tapping the bottom of the ramekins. Bring a medium saucepan of water to a boil. In a medium-sized heat-resistant bowl, combine chocolate, butter, vanilla, coffee, and wine. Place over boiling water and reduce heat to a simmer. Whisk chocolate mix until completely melted and all the ingredients are well combined. Remove from heat. Slowly whisk in egg yolks one at a time, being careful not to scramble them. In a separate bowl, add cream of tartar and pinch of salt to egg whites and beat to stiff peaks. Take ¼ of the egg whites and whisk into the chocolate mixture to lighten the mix. Slowly pour the chocolate down the side of the bowl of egg whites and fold gently until completely combined. Do not pour the chocolate directly on top of the whites or you will deflate them. Spoon the soufflé mix into the ramekins, dividing all of the mix evenly among the four ramekins. Place in the oven and reduce heat to 375 degrees. Bake approximately 20 minutes or until the soufflés are puffed and no longer jiggly on top. Serve immediately with crème anglaise and dusted with powdered sugar.

Crème Anglaise

This is a vanilla custard cream that will knock your socks off. It makes more than you need for four souffles, but it'll surely get used up. It is great on chocolate ice cream, delicious as a creamer in coffee, and a fabulous alternative to syrup for pancakes.

YIELDS APPROXIMATELY 1½ CUPS SAUCE

2 cups whole milk	**4 large egg yolks**
¼ cup granulated sugar	**2 Tbsp ChocoVine**
2 tsp pure vanilla extract	

In a medium-sized saucepan over medium heat, combine the milk and the vanilla and bring to a simmer. Remove from heat. In a separate bowl, whisk egg yolks with sugar until well combined and pale yellow. Slowly pour the milk into the yolk/sugar mix, whisking constantly to combine so as not to scramble the eggs. Transfer custard back into the saucepan and place on medium-low heat, stirring constantly until the sauce begins to thicken enough to thinly coat the back of a wooden spoon. Don't overcook or the sauce will scramble. Remove from heat and add ChocoVine. Pour sauce through a fine sieve into a bowl sitting in an ice water bath. Let the sauce cool completely before covering with plastic wrap and putting in the refrigerator. Sauce can be made up to 5 days in advance and kept covered and chilled.

Homemade Fruit Sorbet

This recipe works great with virtually any fresh fruit in season. It is a healthy alternative to ice cream and keeps very well in an airtight container. If you do not have fresh fruit, you can substitute frozen fruit. Let the fruit thaw before placing in the food processor or you may damage the motor or blade.

YIELD:

1 cup water
1 cup granulated sugar
1 cup fruit (raspberry and strawberry are personal favorites)

1 tsp lemon juice
1 tsp vanilla extract
1 tsp ground cinnamon

Combine water and sugar in a microwaveable bowl. Microwave the mixture for 7 minutes, stirring halfway through. Place fruit, lemon juice, cinnamon, and vanilla in a food processor. Purée. Add water/sugar mix. Purée again. Strain mixture through a fine mesh sieve, stirring with a wooden spoon to remove any peel or seeds. Place sorbet into an airtight container and put in the freezer. Stir every 30 minutes for 3 hours. Allow sorbet to sit in the freezer overnight to set.

Wine and Cheese Party

Hosting a wine and cheese party is one of the most laid back approaches to entertaining. It involves minimal preparation, minimal cost and maximum fun. I like to use wine and cheese parties as learning experiences, an opportunity to discover new wines and cheeses that I haven't had a chance to sample yet.

The rule of thumb is to do a good assortment of soft cheeses, semi-soft cheeses, semi-hard cheeses and hard cheeses. If all you are serving is cheese, perhaps 5 or 6 different options is adequate, served alongside fruit, nuts and gluten-free rice crackers or nut thins. The accompaniments are necessary as palate cleansers between the cheeses. They enable you to really maximize your tasting experience while also providing you with something of substance to eat with the wine.

Generally speaking you would want to serve sweeter wines along with milder, softer cheeses and more aggressive dry wines with stronger, harder, more aggressive cheeses. A fun way of pairing the wines along with the cheeses is to match wines with cheeses based upon the country of origin. By doing so you can really taste what the French call "terroir" or the earth that gives each wine and cheese its unique flavor profile. Just like grapes can taste completely different based on the micro-climate they grow in, so too can cheese based upon the particular diets of the animals from a particular micro-climate. It's all about the soil, the earth, the "terroir."

A couple of warnings about cheese with regard to a gluten-free lifestyle. Cheeses in general are safe as long as they are not processed. However, brie and camembert or any cheese that has been aged by coating it with a layer of flour is off limits. Historically speaking blue cheeses and gorgonzolas were also considered to be off limits, but more recent research has shown that these are no longer a risk. To be on the safe side though, it is worth staying away from them so that you don't take any chances. There are plenty of other incredible options for cheeses that are guaranteed safe. A fantastic resource for gourmet cheeses is www.igourmet.com. You can order online and have cheeses shipped to you from all over the world in refrigerated packages overnight. It is convenient and you'll certainly find a selection unlike most other places unless you happen to live in a metropolitan area that has a specialty cheese shop or cheese monger.

Here is a sample Cheese and Wine Menu that you can use as a guideline. Remember, be creative. There is a whole world of cheeses out there to be had. Don't pigeonhole yourself into good old standbys. And don't be afraid of strong smelling cheeses. Usually the more intense the smell of a cheese, the more incredible the flavor.

First Course: Manouri: Soft Greek cheese made from sheep's milk. Pair with Moschofilero Boutari wine.

Second Course: Carr Valley Cocoa Cardona: Semi-soft cheese from Wisconsin made of goat's milk. Pair with Schramsberg Blanc de Blancs sparkling wine.

Third Course: Australian Aussie Jack: Semi-hard cheese made from cow's milk. Pair with a Gibson Shiraz.

Fourth Course: French Mimolette Jeune: Semi-hard cow's milk cheese that dates back to the time of King Louis the 14th. Pair with Bourgogne Pinot Noir Guy Chaumont.

Fifth Course: Extra Aged Manchego: Spanish hard cheese made with sheep's milk. Pair with Protos Tempranillo wine.

Afterword

As a health professional, I encounter many persons with gluten intolerance that experience great anxiety about preparing foods properly to avoid any symptoms or gastrointestinal discomfort. This gluten-free cookbook offers some creative solutions to gluten-free food preparation. Many of these recipes can be adapted for multiple environments including hospital stays and entertaining in the home. It is extremely helpful that these recipes specify safe brand names to ensure the contents are gluten-free.

I like the fact that there are no "substitutions" in the ingredients since all recipes are designed to be gluten-free. And with the variety of foods and tasty seasonings, most any person is apt to enjoy these deliciously created dishes, so there will be no need to make separate meals. For special occasions, there are holiday and culturally diverse menus and recipes. What a great entertaining resource!

Since we currently see 1 in every 133 Americans as positive for Celiac Disease or Gluten Enteropathy, there is an increasing need for safe and easy-to-use food preparation resources, such as this gluten-free cookbook. This book proves that gluten-free cooking can be tasty, nutritious, diverse and easy to produce. Happy, safe eating!

Debra L. Tindle, RD
System Clinical
Nutrition Manager,
Orange County, CA
Morrison Management
Specialists

Index

Flourless Chocolate Cake with Fresh
    Raspberries and Raspberry Sauce,
    176
Fruit Sorbet, 182
Indian Spiced Rice Pudding, 98
Macerated Strawberries with
    Balsamic Reduction and
    Mascarpone Cream, 155
Majoun, 56
Mexican Style Chocolate Mousse,
    178
Ricotta Cheesecake with Raspberry
    Sauce, 86
Sweet Potato Pots de Crèmes, 160
Zabaglione with Fresh Fruit, 78

Dips
Caramelized Onion and Garlic Dip,
    29
Grilled Corn and Black Bean Salsa,
    89
Guacamole, 88
Hungarian Paprika Dip, 33
Spinach and Artichoke Dip, 35

Eggs
Broccoli, Sun-Dried Tomato and
    Goat Cheese Frittata, 166
Gâteau D'Omelettes avec Pipérades
    et Champignons, 110, 112
Green Eggs and Ham, 38
Hungarian Style Deviled Eggs
    (Casino Eggs), 28
Individual Egg and Cheese Souffles,
    168

Fish
Fish en Papillote with Julienne
    Vegetables (Fish in Parchment
    Paper), 154
Tuna and Rice Salad, 42

Fruits
Fruit Sorbet, 182
Macerated Strawberries with
    Balsamic Reduction and
    Mascarpone Cream, 155
Mixed Greens with Chèvre, Candied

Pecans, Pear, and Champagne Wine
    Vinaigrette, 102
Moroccan Fruit Salad, 64
Poached Pears in a Port or Marsala
    and Orange Sauce, 139
Zabaglione with Fresh Fruit, 78

Garnishes
Balsamic Reduction, 40
Candied Pecans, 103
Créme Fraîche, 101
Mascarpone Cream, 140
Tapenade, 40

Lamb
Lamb Köfte with Tomato Coulis, 54

Meats — see Beef, Lamb, Pork

Pasta
Crispy Pancetta, Smoked Gouda and
    Gruyère Mac and Cheese, 172
Pastitsio, 70

Pork
Albóndigas Soup, 90
Maple Glazed Pork Loin, 158
Paprika Pork Ribs, 43
Pork or Beef Taquitos, 91

Poultry — see Chicken

Rice
Goat Cheese Risotto, 138
Rizopita, 72

Salads
Carrot Raita, 96
Cucumber Raita, 95
Feta, Tomato, and Preserved Lemon
    Salad, 63
Grilled Vegetable Napoleon with
    Roasted Garlic Aioli, Sopressata
    Crisp, Parmesan Tuile, and
    Balsamic Reduction, 80
Iceberg Wedge with Green Goddess
    Dressing, 172
Mixed Bean Salad — Palikaria, 144

Standard Measurements:

a pinch ..... 1/8 tsp or less
3 teaspoons ..... 1 Tablespoon
4 Tablespoons ..... 1/4 cup
8 Tablespoons ..... 1/2 cup
12 Tablespoons ..... 3/4 cup
16 Tablespoons ..... 1 cup
2 cups ..... 1 pint
2 pints ..... 1 quart
4 quarts ..... 1 gallon
1 ounce ..... 2 Tablespoons
8 ounces ..... 1 cup
16 ounces ..... 1 pound

All measurements are level.